F*CK
THAT'S
HOT!

60 recipes to up the heat in the kitchen

F*CK THAT'S HOT!

Billy Law

Smith
Street
Books

FEELING

F*CK THA

MELTDOW

THE HEAT'S ON!

Don't play with chillies or you might get burned ...

Yep, this cookbook is all about chillies: the hot, the super hot and the 'oh my God my insides are on fire and I literally might die' hot. No amount of spice has been left unturned in this collection of mouth-numbing recipes. From Malaysia's curry laksa, Jamaica's jerk chicken and India's beef vindaloo, to fire-laden nachos and, of course, the world's hottest curry the ferocious phaal, I have scoured the globe to bring you the hottest, spiciest and most chilli-laden dishes from this side of the Milky Way. So, if you are ready to sweat, cry and take up the challenge of a full chilli meltdown, then this is the cookbook you've been waiting for.

Chilli, pepper or chilli pepper, whatever you want to call it, this pocket rocket is the one spice that many of us just can't live without. The humble chilli plant (*Capsicum annuum*) is a member of the nightshade family originating from Mexico, and its fruit has been a part of the human diet for at least 9000 years, with cultivation beginning in northeastern Mexico from at least 5500 years ago. It stayed that way for 5000 years until Christopher Columbus and his crew reached the Caribbean, where they became the first Europeans to encounter 'capsicums', calling them 'peppers' because the chillies had a hot, spicy, taste like black peppercorns. The chilli was among the many ingredients Columbus took back to Spain, along with tomatoes, avocados, potatoes, sweetcorn, pumpkin and chocolate among others, and from there the plant spread to the rest of Europe where it became a popular and indispensable spice in many of Europe's most famous cuisines. Its journey didn't end there, however, and soon the chilli was bound for Asia, accompanying Portuguese traders in the 15th century to India and then on to Southeast Asia and China, where it became such a fundamental part of the diet it's almost impossible to imagine a cuisine from this region without the addition of this ubiquitous spice. Nowadays, of course, chillies are everywhere and there are perhaps as many types of chilli as there are dishes that include them. From snacks sold on the streets of Bangkok to some of the most sophisticated dishes found in the world's finest restaurants, the chilli is ever-present, adding flavour, warmth and that familiar fuzziness we all can't get enough of.

Like most people, I adore chillies and like many kids who grew up in Southeast Asia, I was trained to enjoy spicy food from a very young age. Where I come from in Malaysia, we are absolutely addicted to chilli, so much so that we will always find a way to add heat to whatever we are eating. This might be as simple as adding a small dollop of sambal belachan to the Malaysian national dish nasi lemak, throwing a good handful of chillies into a satay sauce, or adding them to a traditional rempah spice paste to make chicken curry. As I've grown older, my lifelong appreciation for hot and spicy food has also grown. That doesn't necessarily mean I always chase after the hottest dish, but I love learning more about the beauty of chillies and how they can elevate the flavours of different recipes.

The chapters in this cookbook are categorised by spice level: Feeling the Heat, F*ck that's Hot and Meltdown! Let this be your guide, but remember we all have different heat-tolerance levels, so you may find that some recipes are mild, while others may blow your head off. I encourage you to experiment and adjust the heat level in each recipe to suit your palate. You don't need to be a hero and go all gung-ho with the chillies – just give the really hot versions to your mates instead. And remember, what goes in must come out. You've been warned!

KNOW YOU

Poblano

Bullhorn green

Thai scud

Carolina reaper

R CHILLIES

Piquanté pepper

Bullhorn yellow

Long green

Bullhorn red

Bird's-eye

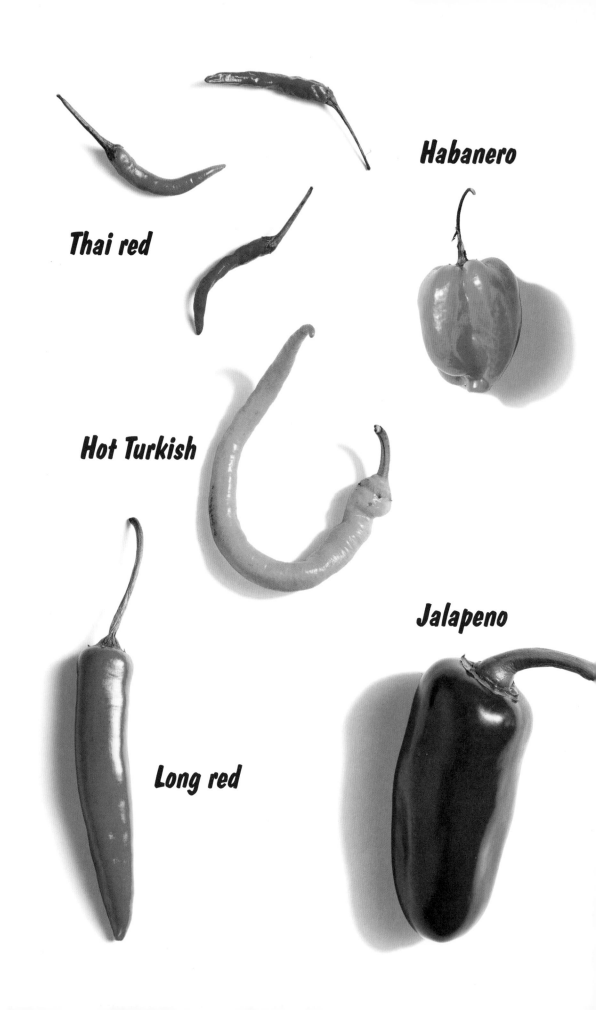

Habanero

Thai red

Hot Turkish

Jalapeno

Long red

SCOVILLE HEAT UNITS

15 million	Capsaicin
2.5 million	Dragon's breath
2 million	Carolina reaper
1 million	Ghost pepper
500,000	Chocolate habanero
250,000	Scotch bonnet
200,000	Orange habanero
100,000	Thai
50,000	Tabasco
40,000	Cayenne
20,000	Serrano
10,000	Aleppo
5,000	Jalapeno
2,500	Guajillo
2,000	Poblano
1,500	Ancho
1,000	Piquanté
500	Paprika
0	Capsicum (Bell pepper)

BACON-WRAPPED JALAPENO
POPPERS

Don't be a party pooper; instead, make these jalapeno party poppers! They're the perfect finger food for your next game night or dinner party. They are super easy to prepare and are usually gone within seconds, so make a double batch. If you want to be a cheeky devil, hide a habanero popper in the pile and wait to see who gets bombed!

Makes 24

220 g (8 oz) cream cheese

30 g (1 oz) soft blue cheese, such as Gorgonzola or Roquefort

½ teaspoon cayenne pepper

½ teaspoon freshly ground black pepper

½ teaspoon sea salt

12 jalapeno chillies, halved and deseeded

12 thin slices bacon, halved crossways

Preheat the oven to 220°C (430°F). Line a large baking tray with baking paper.

Combine the cream cheese, blue cheese, cayenne pepper, black pepper and salt in a mixing bowl. Carefully spoon the mixture into the jalapeno halves, then wrap a bacon slice around each half to enclose the filling. Secure the bacon with toothpicks and place on the prepared tray.

Bake in the oven for 20–25 minutes, until the bacon is crispy and the cheese has melted.

SICHUAN-STYLE MIXED NUTS

Do you like your nuts hot and spicy? These nuts are not only spicy from the dried chillies, but the Sichuan peppercorns will give you a hot, tingling, numbing sensation on the lips. They're highly addictive, so I suggest you go nuts and double the quantity.

○ ○

Makes about 300 g (10½ oz)

160 g (5½ oz/1 cup) raw peanuts, skins removed
160 g (5½ oz/1 cup) raw cashews
80 g (2¾ oz/½ cup) raw almonds
50 g (1¾ oz/½ cup) pecans
2 tablespoons unsalted butter, melted

Sichuan spice mix
1 tablespoon vegetable oil
1 tablespoon Sichuan peppercorns
10 small dried chillies
1 teaspoon Chinese five spice powder
½ teaspoon ground white pepper
2 teaspoons caster (superfine) sugar
2 teaspoons sea salt

Preheat the oven to 180°C (350°F). Line a large baking tray with baking paper.

To make the Sichuan spice mix, heat the vegetable oil in a frying pan over medium heat and sauté the Sichuan peppercorns and dried chillies for 2–3 minutes, until very fragrant (you might want to have the windows open as the chilli fumes can be overpowering).

Using a wire-mesh strainer or similar, scoop the peppercorns and chillies onto paper towel to soak up the excess oil and leave to cool slightly. Place half the peppercorns and chillies in a mortar and pestle or spice grinder and roughly pound or grind into flakes. Transfer to a large bowl and add the remaining spice mix ingredients, along with the remaining whole peppercorns and chillies.

Add all the nuts and the melted butter to the spice mix and stir until well coated. Spread the nuts on the prepared tray in a single layer and bake in the oven for 10–15 minutes, tossing once at the halfway mark, until the nuts are toasted and slightly golden.

Set the spicy nuts aside to cool completely, then transfer to an airtight container where they will keep in the pantry for up to 2 weeks.

HUEVOS RANCHEROS

This dish may be called 'ranchers' eggs' due to it being the typical breakfast served on Mexican farms, but it is also the perfect hangover cure after a big night out. And for those who are extra hungover, just add bacon and sausages to make you feel a whole new you.

Serves 4

1 tablespoon extra virgin olive oil
1 large onion, finely diced
1 jalapeno chilli, deseeded and
 thinly sliced
2 garlic cloves, finely chopped
handful of coriander (cilantro) leaves,
 roughly chopped, plus extra
 to serve
400 g (14 oz) tin diced tomatoes
sea salt
4 free-range eggs
4 corn tortillas
50 g (1¾ oz/½ cup) grated cheddar
Siracha hot sauce (optional; see
 page 158 or use store-bought)

Refried beans
2 teaspoons extra virgin olive oil
1 onion, finely diced
400 g (14 oz) tin black beans, rinsed
 and drained
¼ teaspoon cayenne pepper
sea salt and freshly ground
 black pepper

Heat half the oil in a large frying pan over medium–high heat. Add the onion, jalapeno and garlic and sauté for 2 minutes or until the onion has softened. Stir through the coriander and tomatoes, then reduce the heat to medium–low and simmer, stirring occasionally, for 8–10 minutes, until the sauce has reduced and thickened. Taste and season with salt.

Meanwhile, to make the refried beans, heat the oil in a saucepan over medium heat. Add the onion and sauté for 2 minutes or until soft and translucent. Add the beans and 60 ml (2 fl oz/¼ cup) water, then cover and cook, stirring occasionally, for 5 minutes.

Using a potato masher or a fork, lightly mash the beans, then season with the cayenne pepper and salt and pepper. Stir well to combine, reduce the heat to low and cook for a further 2–3 minutes, until thickened. Set aside and keep warm.

Heat the remaining oil in a frying pan over medium heat and fry the eggs, sunny side up. Set the eggs aside on a plate, then add the tortillas to the pan, reduce the heat to medium–low and warm the tortillas, flipping regularly, until just starting to crisp at the edges.

To serve, spread the refried beans over the tortillas, then top with a few spoonfuls of the tomato sauce, followed by a fried egg. Sprinkle with grated cheddar and extra coriander, and drizzle over some sriracha for those who like it extra hot.

CHANA MASALA

This vegetarian dish is both healthy and packed full of flavour. Chana masala is a staple in many Indian households because it's easy to make and chickpeas are an excellent source of protein. It is often my go-to dish whenever I need to whip up a quick, simple meal. Any leftovers become even more flavoursome if left overnight, making it perfect for lunch the next day.

Serves 4–6

3–4 garlic cloves, roughly chopped
2 tablespoons freshly grated ginger
2–3 long green chillies, thinly sliced
1 large onion, finely diced
sea salt
2 tablespoons ghee or vegetable oil
1 teaspoon cumin seeds
2 teaspoons black mustard seeds
1 tablespoon ground coriander
½ teaspoon chilli powder
1 teaspoon ground turmeric
1 teaspoon garam masala
400 g (14 oz) tin puréed or
 diced tomatoes
2 x 400 g (14 oz) tins chickpeas, rinsed
 and drained
2 tablespoons freshly squeezed
 lemon juice, plus lemon wedges
 to serve
handful of coriander (cilantro) leaves,
 to garnish (optional)
steamed basmati rice or warm
 paratha, to serve

Combine the garlic, ginger, green chilli, onion and a pinch of salt in a blender and blitz to a fine paste.

Heat the ghee or vegetable oil in a large saucepan over medium-high heat. Add the cumin and mustard seeds and sauté for 10–15 seconds, until fragrant. Add the blended onion mixture and cook, stirring occasionally, for 8–10 minutes, until completely softened and the oil has started to render out.

Add the ground coriander, chilli powder, turmeric and garam masala and cook, stirring, for 2 minutes. If the mixture becomes too dry, add 1 tablespoon water and scrape the bottom of the pan to dislodge any caramelised bits.

Add the tomatoes and chickpeas, then season with salt and stir to combine. Bring the mixture to the boil and add 125 ml (4 fl oz/½ cup) water if the mixture is very dry. Reduce the heat to low and simmer, stirring occasionally, for 15–20 minutes, until the curry has reduced to a thick stew. Taste and adjust the seasoning accordingly.

Remove the pan from the heat and stir in the lemon juice. Divide the chana masala among bowls, garnish with coriander leaves (if using) and serve with steamed basmati rice or warm paratha and lemon wedges for squeezing over.

SPICY SRI LANKAN VEG CURRY

Curry is a simple way to add tons of flavour to vegetables. This Sri Lankan vegetable curry is a one-pot wonder, perfect for mid-week meals and feeding the family. If you like, go fancy with the vegetables and mix it up by adding eggplant (aubergine), okra or snake (yard-long) beans.

Serves 4–6

2 tablespoons vegetable oil
1 teaspoon cumin seeds
1 teaspoon fennel seeds
1 teaspoon black mustard seeds
2 green cardamom pods, smashed
5 whole cloves
½ cinnamon stick, broken into
    small pieces
1 large onion, finely diced
2 long green chillies, thinly sliced
    diagonally
1 teaspoon chilli powder
1 teaspoon ground turmeric
1 teaspoon ground coriander
1 teaspoon all-purpose curry powder
1 teaspoon garam masala
300 g (10½ oz) cauliflower, broken into
    small florets
2 carrots, cut into small dice
200 g (7 oz) green beans, trimmed and
    cut into 3 cm (1¼ in) lengths
2 potatoes, cut into small dice
400 ml (13½ fl oz) tin coconut milk
80 g (2¾ oz/½ cup) frozen peas
sea salt and freshly ground
    black pepper
steamed basmati rice or warm naan
    bread, to serve

Heat the oil in a wok or large frying pan over medium heat. Add the cumin, fennel and mustard seeds, cardamom pods, cloves and cinnamon and sauté for 30 seconds or until fragrant. Add the onion and green chilli and sauté for 3 minutes or until the onion is soft and translucent. Add the chilli powder, turmeric, coriander, curry powder and garam masala and cook for 1 minute or until fragrant.

Add the cauliflower, carrot, green beans and potato and stir into the spice mixture until they are nicely coated. Cook for 2 minutes or until the vegetables are just starting to soften. Pour in the coconut milk and just enough water to cover the vegetables. Increase the heat to medium–high and bring to the boil. Reduce the heat to medium–low and simmer for 10 minutes or until the vegetables are cooked through. Add the peas and cook for 5 minutes or until the curry sauce has thickened slightly. Taste and season with salt and pepper.

Serve the curry with steamed basmati rice or warm naan bread to mop up that delicious curry sauce.

MAPO TOFU

Mapo tofu is one of the most popular Sichuan dishes for chilli aficionados. This dish highlights the complexity of Sichuan cuisine's 'mala' flavours (meaning 'numbingly spicy'), by using flavourless bean curd to soak up the aromatic chilli sauce.

Serves 2

120 g (4½ oz) minced (ground) pork
2 teaspoons Shaoxing rice wine
1 teaspoon light soy sauce
½ teaspoon grated ginger
1 tablespoon vegetable oil
2 teaspoons Sichuan peppercorns, plus extra, ground, to serve
2 dried chillies, cut into 1 cm (½ in) lengths
2 tablespoons doubanjiang (see Note)
2 teaspoons Sichuan chilli oil (see page 157)
¼ teaspoon Chinese five spice powder
1 teaspoon sugar
400 g (14 oz) firm silken tofu, cut into 2.5 cm (1 in) cubes
2 teaspoons cornflour (corn starch) mixed with 1 tablespoon water
1 spring onion (scallion), thinly sliced
steamed rice, to serve

Combine the minced pork, Shaoxing rice wine, soy sauce and ginger in a bowl. Mix well and set aside.

Heat the oil in a wok or large frying pan over medium–high heat. Add the Sichuan peppercorns and dried chilli and quickly stir-fry for 15 seconds or until fragrant and the peppercorns are crispy and dark brown in colour. Skim the spices out using a wire-mesh strainer or similar and discard.

Add the minced pork mixture to the hot oil and stir-fry for 2 minutes or until browned and crispy. Add the doubanjiang, chilli oil, Chinese five spice powder and sugar and stir-fry for another minute. Stir through 250 ml (8½ fl oz/1 cup) water and bring to the boil. Gently slide the tofu into the bubbling broth, then reduce the heat to medium, stir once and simmer for 8–10 minutes, until the sauce has reduced by half.

Pour the cornflour mixture into the pan, add the spring onion and gently stir through the mixture without breaking the tofu.

Divide the mapo tofu between bowls and sprinkle over a little ground Sichuan peppercorn. Serve with steamed rice on the side.

Note: Doubanjiang is a fermented spicy broad bean paste widely used in Sichuan cuisine. Usually there are two types: spicy and non-spicy. Obviously we opted for the spicy version.

SHIT-HOT SHAKSHUKA

If you have an upcominig camping trip or a group of friends staying over for the weekend, this breakfast dish is ideal for feeding hungry mouths. Originating from North Africa, but most commonly known as a popular Israeli dish, Shakshuka is a big one-pan mash-up of tomatoes, aromatic herbs and spices and poached eggs that's perfect for sharing.

Serves 4–6

1 tablespoon olive oil, plus extra
   for drizzling
1 large onion, finely diced
1 red capsicum (bell pepper), thinly
   sliced
1 jalapeno or red habanero chilli,
   deseeded and finely chopped
3 garlic cloves, finely chopped
1 teaspoon ground cumin
1 teaspoon smoked paprika
400 g (14 oz) tin diced tomatoes
sea salt and freshly ground
   black pepper
6 free-range eggs
handful of parsley leaves
35 g (1¼ oz/¼ cup) crumbled
   feta (optional)
crusty bread, to serve

Heat the olive oil in a large frying pan over medium–high heat. Add the onion, capsicum and chilli and sauté for 5 minutes or until the onion is soft and beginning to brown. Add the garlic, cumin and paprika and sauté for 2 minutes or until fragrant. Add the tomatoes and 125 ml (4 fl oz/½ cup) water to the pan and stir to mix well. Taste and season with salt and pepper, then reduce the heat to medium–low and bring to a simmer.

Crack the eggs into the pan and spread them out evenly on top of the sauce. Cover and cook for 6–8 minutes, until the eggs are just cooked through but still runny.

Sprinkle the parsley and feta (if using) over the top of the shakshuka, drizzle with extra olive oil and serve in the pan with crusty bread on the side.

29

JAMBALAYA

Jambalaya is a hearty rice dish hailing from the Deep South of Louisiana with influences from Spanish, West African and French cuisines. It is packed with meaty goodness and is pure comfort food at its best. You can dial up the heat level by adding habanero chillies along with the jalapenos to make it an extra warming winter warmer.

Serves 2

2 tablespoons olive oil, plus extra
    if needed
200 g (7 oz) raw andouille or chorizo
    sausage, cut diagonally into 1 cm
    (½ in) thick slices
450 g (1 lb) boneless skinless chicken
    thighs, cut into bite-sized chunks
1 large onion, finely diced
1 celery stalk, diced
1 green capsicum (bell pepper), diced
5 garlic cloves, finely chopped
2 jalapeno chillies, finely diced
300 g (10½/1½ cups) long-grain white
    rice, rinsed and drained
¼ teaspoon dried chilli flakes
¼ teaspoon cayenne pepper
2 tablespoons Cajun or Creole
    seasoning, plus extra if needed
400 g (14 oz) tin crushed tomatoes
750 ml (25½ fl oz/3 cups) chicken stock
2 bay leaves
450 g (1 lb) large raw prawns (shrimp),
    peeled and deveined
50 g (1¾ oz) young okra, thinly sliced
sea salt and freshly ground black pepper
1 spring onion (scallion), thinly sliced
roughly chopped parsley leaves, to
    garnish
Tabasco sauce, to serve

Heat the olive oil in a large heavy-based saucepan or flameproof casserole dish over medium–high heat. Add the sausage and cook, stirring, for 5 minutes or until browned. Remove the sausage from the pan and set aside on a plate. Add the chicken to the pan and cook, stirring frequently, for 8–10 minutes, until well browned on all sides. Set the chicken aside with the sausage.

Add a little more oil to the pan if necessary, then sauté the onion, celery, capsicum, garlic and jalapeno for 3–5 minutes, until fragrant and the onion is soft and translucent.

Tip the chicken and sausage, along with any juices, back into the pan, then add the rice and stir well to combine. Stir through the chilli flakes, cayenne pepper, Cajun or Creole seasoning, crushed tomatoes and chicken stock and bring to the boil. Add the bay leaves, then reduce the heat to medium–low, cover and cook, stirring occasionally, for 20–25 minutes, until the rice has absorbed most of the stock. Add the prawns and okra, stir gently, then cover again and simmer for a further 5–10 minutes, until the prawns are plump and pink and the rice is cooked through.

Taste and season with salt and pepper, along with more Cajun or Creole seasoning, if necessary, to suit your taste. Garnish with the spring onion and parsley, and serve immediately with Tabasco sauce for an extra kick.

BLAZING BUTTER CHICKEN

While many of us are accustomed to butter chicken being a mild curry dish, this recipe raises the heat level just a little to match how they serve it in New Delhi, India. Once you have tasted this version, I don't think you will go back. Make sure to serve it with plenty of warm naan to mop up the awesome buttery curry sauce.

Serves 4

1 kg (2 lb 3 oz) boneless skinless chicken thighs, cut into large chunks

400 g (14 oz) tin diced tomatoes

5 garlic cloves

5 cm (2 in) knob of ginger, peeled and sliced

2 long green chillies, thickly sliced

20 g (¾ oz) raw cashews, soaked in hot water for 15 minutes, then drained, plus extra chopped cashews to garnish

3 tablespoons butter

1 tablespoon Kashmiri chilli powder

1 teaspoon regular chilli powder

2 teaspoons garam masala

1 teaspoon ground coriander

1 teaspoon ground cumin

½ teaspoon ground cardamom

250 ml (8½ fl oz/1 cup) thick (double/ heavy) cream

1 teaspoon sea salt

Place the chicken and all the marinade ingredients in a large bowl and mix until the chicken is nicely coated. Cover and set aside in the fridge to marinate for at least 1 hour, but preferably overnight.

Preheat a barbecue grill to high.

Grill the chicken for 2–3 minutes on each side until slightly charred at the edges. Transfer the chicken to a tray, cover with foil and keep warm.

Place the tomatoes, garlic, ginger, green chilli and cashews in a blender and blitz to a purée.

Melt 2 tablespoons of the butter in a large saucepan over medium–high heat. Once sizzling, add the chilli powders, garam masala and ground spices and sauté for 10 seconds or until fragrant. Stir through the puréed tomato mixture and bring to a simmer. Reduce the heat to medium–low and simmer, stirring occasionally, for 30 minutes or until the sauce has an almost paste-like consistency and is reddish brown in colour.

Add the cream, salt and sugar to the pan and stir to mix well. Add the seared chicken along with all the juice on the tray, then sprinkle in the kasoori methi by rubbing the leaves between your palms over the chicken. Stir, then cover and simmer for 10 minutes or until the chicken is cooked through.

1 tablespoon sugar
½ teaspoon kasoori methi (see Note)
coriander (cilantro) leaves, to garnish
steamed basmati rice and warm naan
    bread, to serve

<u>Butter chicken marinade</u>
3 garlic cloves, minced
3 cm (1¼ in) knob of ginger, minced
125 g (4½ oz/½ cup) Greek yoghurt
2 teaspoons Kashmiri chilli powder
1 teaspoon garam masala
1 teaspoon ground coriander
1 teaspoon ground turmeric
1 teaspoon chilli powder
1 teaspoon sea salt

Add the remaining butter to the pan and stir until it has melted and
the sauce is thick and luxurious. Sprinkle the chopped cashews
and coriander leaves over the top and serve with steamed basmati
rice and warm naan bread on the side.

*Note: Kasoori methi are crushed fenugreek leaves and should not be mistaken for
fenugreek seeds. In Indian cuisine, kasoori methi is commonly added at the end of
cooking to elevate the flavour of curries. You can purchase it at any Indian grocers
and some supermarkets.*

SICHUAN-STYLE EGGPLANT

'Yu xiang' is a famous seasoning in Sichuan cuisine. Despite the term literally meaning 'fish fragrance' in Chinese, this popular eggplant (aubergine) dish actually contains no seafood. The harmonious balance of salty, sweet, sour and spicy in the sauce really makes the eggplant sing, making it so much more than just a naughty emoji.

Serves 4 as a side dish

3 long (about 600 g/1 lb 5 oz) Chinese eggplants (aubergines)
sea salt
2 tablespoons vegetable oil
1 teaspoon Sichuan peppercorns, coarsely crushed
2 bird's eye chillies, thinly sliced
2 tablespoons doubanjiang (see Note on page 26)
4 garlic cloves, finely chopped
2.5 cm (1 in) knob of ginger, grated
1 spring onion (scallion), thinly sliced
handful of coriander (cilantro) leaves, roughly chopped (optional)
steamed jasmine rice, to serve

Yu xiang sauce
1 teaspoon light soy sauce
2 tablespoons Shaoxing rice wine
1 tablespoon Chinese black vinegar
2 teaspoons cornflour (corn starch)
1 tablespoon sugar

Cut the eggplants in half, then cut each half into quarters. Place the eggplant on a baking tray, skin side down, and lightly sprinkle salt over the top. Set aside for 20 minutes to allow the eggplant to sweat out some of its juices, then rinse and pat dry with paper towel.

Meanwhile, combine the yu xiang sauce ingredients in a small bowl. Set aside.

Heat the vegetable oil in a wok or large frying pan over high heat until smoking. Add the eggplant and stir-fry for 2–3 minutes, until the eggplant is soft and starting to brown on all sides. Add the Sichuan peppercorns, chilli, doubanjiang, garlic and ginger and stir-fry for 1 minute or until fragrant.

Give the yu xiang sauce a quick stir and pour over the eggplant. Reduce the heat to medium and gently stir until the eggplant is nicely coated in the sauce. Taste and adjust the seasoning if necessary. Simmer for 1 minute or until the sauce thickens and becomes glossy.

Transfer the eggplant to a serving dish, sprinkle over the spring onion and coriander leaves (if using) and serve with steamed jasmine rice on the side.

SRIRACHA AND HONEY CHICKEN WINGS

These sweet and spicy wings are always a crowd pleaser. Don't be alarmed by the amount of baking powder in this recipe, it is the crucial 'secret ingredient' to making the wings extra crispy and it won't leave that soapy, bitter aftertaste. The only thing you do need to worry about is where to put your sticky fingers.

Serves 2–4

1 kg (2 lb 3 oz) chicken wingettes or drumettes
1 tablespoon sea salt
1 teaspoon smoked paprika
1 teaspoon cayenne pepper
1 teaspoon freshly ground black pepper
2 tablespoons baking powder
1 spring onion (scallion), thinly sliced (optional)
toasted unsalted peanuts, roughly chopped, to serve (optional)

Honey & sriracha glaze
90 g (3 oz/¼ cup) honey
80 ml (2½ fl oz/⅓ cup) Sriracha hot sauce (see page 158 or use store-bought), plus extra to serve
1 tablespoon fish sauce
juice of ½ lime
1 teaspoon sesame oil

Preheat the oven to 220°C (430°F). Place a wire rack over a baking tray lined with baking paper.

Place the chicken in a large bowl, add the salt, paprika, cayenne pepper, black pepper and baking powder and mix everything together until the chicken is nicely coated. Lay the chicken on the wire rack in a single layer with space between each piece. Bake in the oven for 45 minutes to 1 hour, turning the chicken halfway through, until golden brown and crispy.

During the last 5 minutes of cooking, make the honey and sriracha glaze. Place all the ingredients in a wok or large frying pan and cook over medium heat until the mixture has reduced to a thick glaze. Add the crispy chicken to the wok or pan and toss it in the glorious glaze until the chicken is completely coated.

Transfer the chicken to a serving platter, sprinkle over the spring onion and peanuts (if using) and drizzle with extra sriracha for the home run.

HOT CHICKEN MOLE ENCHILADAS

Ask any Mexican and most will have their own family recipe for mole sauce. Some like it mild, while others prefer it spicy (no guesses for which we prefer!). It can be bright ruby red or as dark as squid ink from the addition of dark chocolate, as we have done here. Don't be put off by the length of this recipe; it is actually very straightforward and the end result is a rich, wholesome Mexican meal that will send you into a blissful food coma. Ahhhh ...

Makes 8–10

300 g (10½ oz) skinless chicken
  breast fillet
8–10 x 15 cm (6 in) flour tortillas
½ red onion, thinly sliced
200 g (7 oz) grated cheese, such as
  cheddar or gruyere
50 g (1¾ oz) Cotija cheese, crumbled
coriander (cilantro) leaves, to garnish
lime wedges, to serve

Mole sauce
5 dried ancho chillies
1 tablespoon olive oil
5 garlic cloves, finely chopped
1 large onion, finely chopped
3 tablespoons crunchy peanut butter
2 teaspoons sea salt
1 tablespoon sugar
2 tostadas, crushed (see Note)
100 g (3½ oz) dark chocolate
  (65% cocoa solids), roughly chopped
½ teaspoon ground cinnamon
1 red habanero chilli, finely chopped

Bring a saucepan of water to a rolling boil over medium–high heat. Add the chicken and boil for 15–20 minutes or until the chicken is cooked through. Using a slotted spoon, remove the chicken and set aside to cool. Once cool enough to handle, shred the chicken and set aside.

To make the mole sauce, add the ancho chillies to the same pan of boiling water. Remove the pan from the heat and soak the chillies for 30 minutes or until softened. Strain the chillies, reserving the liquid, then cut off and discard the stems and place the chillies in a blender.

Heat the olive oil in a frying pan over medium–high heat. Add the garlic and onion and sauté for 3 minutes or until the onion is soft and translucent. Add the onion mixture to the blender, along with the peanut butter, salt, sugar, tostadas and 500 ml (17 fl oz/2 cups) of the chicken/chilli soaking water. Blend to a purée.

Pour the purée into a large saucepan and bring to a simmer over medium heat. Add the chocolate, cinnamon and habanero chilli and stir until the chocolate has melted. Simmer for 10 minutes or until the sauce has slightly thickened, then reduce the heat to low and keep the sauce warm.

Preheat the oven to 200°C (400°F).

Pour 250 ml (8½ fl oz/1 cup) of the mole sauce into a 23 x 30 cm (9 x 12 in) baking dish and spread the sauce over the base of the dish.

Place a tortilla on a chopping board, spread a line of mole sauce in the centre, then top with a little of the shredded chicken, onion and grated cheese. Wrap up the tortilla and place in the baking dish. Repeat with the remaining ingredients, leaving a little of the grated cheese to sprinkle over the top of the enchiladas, until the baking dish is nicely packed with rolled enchiladas in a single layer. Pour 250 ml (8½ fl oz/1 cup) of the mole sauce over the centre of the enchiladas, sprinkle with the remaining cheese and bake in the oven for 20 minutes or until the cheese is blisteringly golden. Scatter the Cotija or feta and a few coriander leaves over the top and serve with lime wedges on the side and a spiced-laden michelada to wash it all down with, if you're game.

Note: Tostada means 'toasted' in Spanish, and tostadas are basically fried corn tortillas. If you can't find any, you can fry corn tortillas in hot vegetable oil until crisp, or use tortilla chips instead.

FLAMING MEATBALL SPAGHETTI

This dish is a no brainer. I mean, who doesn't like pasta and spicy meatballs? It is ALWAYS a great idea to make extra meatballs, so you can serve them in a sub or as finger food at parties.

Serves 4–6

3 tablespoons olive oil
1 large onion, finely diced
5 garlic cloves, finely chopped
1 teaspoon dried chilli flakes
1 tablespoon dried Italian herb mix
700 g (1 lb 9 oz) passata (puréed tomatoes)
400 g (14 oz) tin diced tomatoes
sea salt and freshly ground black pepper
500 g (1 lb 2 oz) dried spaghetti
50 g (1¾ oz) parmesan

Flaming meatballs
500 g (1 lb 2 oz) lean minced (ground) beef
1 free-range egg
25 g (¾ oz/¼ cup) dry breadcrumbs
3 garlic cloves, finely chopped
2 teaspoons chilli powder
½ teaspoon cayenne pepper
2 teaspoons dried Italian herb mix
2 teaspoons sea salt
1 teaspoon freshly ground black pepper

To make the flaming meatballs, place all the ingredients in a bowl and use your hand to knead everything together until well combined. Scoop out a tablespoon of the mince mixture and roll it into a golf ball-sized ball. Place the meatball on a tray, then repeat with the remaining mince mixture. Transfer the meatballs to the fridge for about 20 minutes to firm up.

Heat 2 tablespoons of the olive oil in a large frying pan over medium–high heat. Working in batches, cook the meatballs until browned on all sides, then transfer to a plate and set aside.

Add the remaining tablespoon of oil to the same pan, then add the onion and garlic and sauté for 3 minutes or until the onion is soft and translucent. Add the chilli flakes and Italian herb mix and cook for 1–2 minutes, until fragrant. Add the passata and diced tomatoes and bring to the boil. Return the meatballs to the pan, stir to coat in the sauce, then reduce the heat to medium and simmer for 10 minutes or until the meatballs are cooked through. Season to taste with salt and pepper.

Meanwhile, bring a large saucepan of salted water to a rolling boil over high heat. Add the spaghetti and give it a stir, then reduce the heat to medium–high and cook until the pasta is al dente. Drain.

Divide the spaghetti among shallow serving bowls and ladle the meatballs and sauce over the top. Grate the parmesan over the meatballs and serve.

CHILLI-SPIKED
CHICKEN AND CHORIZO PAELLA

Paella is a classic Valencian rice dish sold all over the east coast of Spain. There are countless versions, but one of the most popular is the spicy chicken and chorizo paella. My interpretation is pretty easy to make and darn tasty, too. The secret to a good paella is the crust that forms on the bottom of the rice when it cooks in the pan, known as the 'socarrat'. No crust, no paella!

Serves 4

1 litre (34 fl oz/4 cups) chicken stock
10–15 saffron threads
80 ml (2½ fl oz/⅓ cup) olive oil
500 g (1 lb 2 oz) boneless skinless
   chicken thighs, cut into
   bite-sized pieces
2 raw spicy chorizo sausages, cut
   diagonally into 1 cm (½ in)
   thick slices
3 garlic cloves, finely chopped
1 large onion, finely chopped
300 g (10½ oz) arborio or carnaroli rice
1 teaspoon chilli flakes
½ teaspoon cayenne pepper
2 teaspoons smoked paprika
40 g (1½ oz) tomato paste
   (concentrated purée)
400 g (14 oz) tin diced tomatoes
sea salt
200 g (7 oz) frozen peas

Pour the chicken stock into a saucepan and bring to the boil over high heat. Stir in the saffron, then immediately reduce the heat to low to keep the stock warm.

Heat half the olive oil in a 34 cm (13½ in) paella pan or shallow heavy-based flameproof casserole dish over medium–high heat. Add the chicken and sear for 3 minutes or until browned on all sides. Remove the chicken from the pan and set aside on a plate. Add the chorizo to the pan and cook for 2 minutes or until browned and beginning to crisp, then remove from the pan and set aside with the chicken.

Add the remaining oil to the pan and sauté the garlic and onion for 3 minutes or until the onion is soft and translucent. Add the rice, reduce the heat to medium and stir for 2 minutes or until the rice has soaked up the oil and is slightly translucent. Add the chilli flakes, cayenne pepper, paprika, tomato paste and diced tomatoes, then stir and cook until most of the liquid has evaporated. Return the chicken and chorizo to the pan and stir to combine.

Pour the saffron-infused chicken stock into the pan and spread the rice out evenly to cover the base of the pan. Season with salt and simmer, without stirring, for 10 minutes. Carefully stir the rice, then taste and adjust the seasoning if necessary. Scatter the frozen peas over the top, then reduce the heat to low and simmer for 10–15 minutes, until the rice is cooked through. By this time, most of the liquid will have evaporated and a nice crust should have formed on the base of the pan.

Cover the pan with a lid or a clean tea towel and rest for 5 minutes before serving.

STINGING LAMB
ROGAN JOSH

When it comes to lamb curry, rogan josh is definitely a crowd favourite. Traditionally, the lamb is stewed or braised for hours over low heat until it's tender, but I prefer to slow-cook it in the oven without any fuss, until you can easily pull away the tender and juicy lamb using only a fork.

Serves 8

20 g (¾ oz) dried Kashmiri chillies, deseeded and soaked in hot water for 10 minutes, drained
60 ml (2 fl oz/¼ cup) vegetable oil
300 g (10½ oz) French shallots, finely chopped
4 garlic cloves, minced
2.5 cm (1 in) knob of ginger, minced
1 teaspoon chilli powder
1 teaspoon ground turmeric
1 tablespoon ground coriander
400 g (14 oz) tin crushed tomatoes
1 teaspoon sea salt
1 kg (2 lb 3 oz) boneless lamb shoulder, cut into 5 cm (2 in) chunks
125 g (4½ oz/½ cup) Greek-style yoghurt
coriander (cilantro) leaves, to garnish (optional)
steamed basmati rice and/or warm naan bread, to serve

Rogan josh spice mix
6 whole cloves
2 dried bay leaves
2 black cardamom pods
4 green cardamom pods
1 teaspoon fennel seeds
1 cassia bark or cinnamon stick

Preheat the oven to 150°C (300°F).

Blend the soaked and drained chillies in a blender to a fine paste – you will need about 2 tablespoons for this recipe.

Heat the oil in a large heavy-based flameproof casserole dish over medium heat. Add the spice mix ingredients and cook for 30 seconds or until fragrant. Add the shallot and sauté for 5 minutes or until soft and golden. Add the garlic, ginger, chilli powder, turmeric, ground coriander and chilli paste and cook for 1 minute or until fragrant, then add the tomatoes and salt and stir to combine.

Increase the heat to high, add the lamb to the dish and cook, stirring, for 2–3 minutes until the lamb is seared all over. Reduce the heat to low and add the yoghurt a tablespoon at a time, stirring well after each addition to avoid the yoghurt curdling. If the curry seems dry, add a little water to the dish.

Cover the dish and slow-cook in the oven for at least 2 hours or until the lamb is super tender. Taste and adjust the seasoning, if necessary. Transfer the curry to a serving dish and garnish with coriander leaves (if using). Serve warm with steamed basmati rice and/or warm naan bread.

SPICY GUMBO

Gumbo is a popular dish from North America's Deep South, and it is the official cuisine of Louisiana. Do not mistake it for Jambalaya (see page 30), as gumbo is more like a stew. I like the Creole-style gumbo, which often consists of seafood in a tomato-based broth. Fun fact: the word 'gumbo' likely comes from the Niger–Congo languages word for 'okra', one of the key ingredients in this dish.

Serves 8

100 g (3½ oz) okra
2 tablespoons olive oil
5 garlic cloves, finely chopped
1 onion, finely diced
100 g (3½ oz) red capsicum (bell pepper), roughly chopped
100 g (3½ oz) green capsicum (bell pepper), roughly chopped
1 celery stalk, diced
2 large green chillies (serrano or jalapeno), finely chopped
400 g (14 oz) tin diced tomatoes
2 tablespoons tomato paste (concentrated purée)
3 tablespoons Cajun seasoning
1 teaspoon cayenne pepper
3 tablespoons butter
75 g (2¾ oz/½ cup) plain (all-purpose) flour
1 litre (34 fl oz/4 cups) vegetable stock

Preheat the oven to 200°C (400°F).

Place the okra on a baking tray and roast for 15–20 minutes, until the skins start to char. Set aside to cool, then roughly chop.

Heat the olive oil in a large saucepan over medium–high heat. Add the garlic, onion, red and green capsicum, celery and chilli and sauté for 10 minutes or until the onion is soft and translucent. Add the tomatoes, tomato paste, Cajun seasoning and cayenne pepper, then stir and cook for 2 minutes or until most of the liquid has evaporated.

Push all the vegetables to one side of the pan and melt the butter on the empty side. Sprinkle the flour over the melted butter and stir until the flour and butter are completely combined and there are no clumps of flour remaining. Fold the vegetables into the flour mixture and cook, stirring occasionally, for 2–3 minutes, until the flour mixture is dark brown in colour and almost paste-like. Keep stirring and make sure the flour mixture doesn't burn.

Pour 125 ml (4 fl oz/½ cup) of the vegetable stock at a time into the pan, stirring constantly after each addition to ensure the flour mixture doesn't form lumps, and scraping the base of the pan to release any caramelised stuck-on bits.

200 g (7 oz) cooked andouille or chorizo sausage, cut diagonally into 1 cm (½ in) thick slices

500 g (1 lb 2 oz) large raw prawns (shrimp), peeled and deveined

sea salt and freshly ground black pepper, if needed

3 spring onions (scallions), thinly sliced

steamed white rice, to serve

sautéed collard greens or kale, to serve

Tabasco sauce, to serve (optional)

Add the sausage, prawns and chopped okra to the pan and stir to combine. Cook the gumbo, stirring occasionally, for 3 minutes or until the prawns are pink. Taste and season if necessary.

Transfer the gumbo to a serving dish and top with the spring onion. Serve over steamed white rice with sautéed collard greens or kale on the side, and a few flicks of Tabasco sauce if you dare.

MOROCCAN CHILLI LAMB SHANK TAJINE

Make your Sunday a sharing affair with this Moroccan lamb shank tajine, which is an excellent choice for a dinner party. I like to use lamb shanks over other cuts as it means everyone gets a piece, so no fighting over there please! Just place the tajine in the middle of the dining table and let everyone help themselves.

Serves 4

75 g (2¾ oz/½ cup) plain (all-purpose) flour
1 teaspoon sea salt
1 teaspoon freshly ground black pepper
1 teaspoon sumac, plus extra to garnish
4 lamb shanks, trimmed of excess fat
80 ml (2½ fl oz/⅓ cup) olive oil
5 garlic cloves, minced
1 onion, finely chopped
2 carrots, finely diced
40 g (1½ oz) tomato paste (concentrated purée)
2 tablespoons Harissa (see page 161)
½ teaspoon cayenne pepper
1 teaspoon smoked paprika
1 teaspoon ground cumin
500 ml (17 fl oz/2 cups) vegetable stock
400 g (14 oz) tin diced tomatoes
400 g (14 oz) tin chickpeas, rinsed and drained
finely chopped parsley leaves, to garnish
steamed couscous, to serve

Preheat the oven to 160°C (320°F).

Combine the flour, salt, pepper and sumac in a large bowl. Dredge the lamb shanks in the flour mixture until nicely coated, then shake off the excess flour and place on a tray.

Heat half the olive oil in a tajine or flameproof casserole dish over medium heat. Add the lamb shanks and sear on all sides for 3–5 minutes until browned. Remove the lamb from the dish and set aside.

Add the remaining oil to the dish, then sauté the garlic, onion and carrot for 3 minutes or until the onion is soft and translucent. Add the tomato paste, harissa, cayenne pepper, paprika and cumin, stir well to combine and cook for another minute.

Stir through half the vegetable stock, scraping any caramelised bits off the base of the dish. Add the remaining stock and tomatoes and mix well. Return the shanks to the dish, add the chickpeas and bring to a simmer.

Cover and transfer the dish to a low shelf in the oven and cook, stirring the shanks in the dish every hour, for 4 hours or until the lamb is fall-apart tender.

Taste and adjust the seasoning if necessary and let the tajine rest for 10 minutes. Garnish with parsley and sprinkle a smidgen of sumac over the top. Serve with steamed couscous on the side.

RED-HOT CHICKEN TIKKA MASALA

At most curry houses, chicken tikka masala is usually quite mild, but in this recipe we've raised the heat up a notch. Don't be intimidated by the long list of ingredients, it is actually very easy to make, and all done in one pan. Make sure to serve this with plenty of buttery naan bread to complete your food coma.

Serves 4

500 g (1 lb 2 oz) boneless skinless chicken thighs, cut into bite-sized pieces

80 ml (2½ fl oz/⅓ cup) vegetable oil

3 green cardamom pods

1 black cardamom pod

5 whole cloves

5 cm (2 in) cinnamon stick, broken into shards

1 large onion, finely chopped

3 garlic cloves, minced

2.5 cm (1 in) knob of ginger, grated

1 teaspoon garam masala

1 teaspoon ground coriander

1 teaspoon chilli powder

½ teaspoon ground cumin

½ teaspoon ground turmeric

400 g (14 oz) tin crushed tomatoes

1 teaspoon sea salt

250 ml (8½ fl oz/1 cup) thick (double/heavy) cream

2 tablespoons butter

1 teaspoon kasoori methi

Place the chicken and all the marinade ingredients in a large bowl. Mix until the chicken is well coated, then set aside in the fridge to marinate for at least 3 hours, but preferably overnight.

Heat half the vegetable oil in a large frying pan over medium–high heat. Working in batches, cook the chicken for 3 minutes each side, until well browned. Transfer the chicken to a bowl and set aside.

In the same pan, heat the remaining oil over medium heat. Add the green and black cardamom pods, cloves and cinnamon and fry for 30 seconds or until fragrant. Add the onion and sauté for 3 minutes or until soft and translucent. Add the garlic and ginger and cook for 1 minute or until fragrant, then add the garam masala, ground coriander, chilli powder, cumin and turmeric and sauté for another 30 seconds. Add the tomatoes, salt and 250 ml (8½ fl oz/1 cup) water and bring to the boil over high heat. Once boiling, reduce the heat to medium and simmer, stirring occasionally, for 10–15 minutes, until the sauce thickens and turns a rich dark red.

Pour the curry sauce into a blender and wait 5 minutes for it to cool slightly. Blend the sauce into a purée, then return it to the same pan and stir in the cream. Add the chicken and bring to a simmer over medium heat.

handful of coriander (cilantro) sprigs,
  to garnish
warm naan bread, to serve

<u>Tikka masala marinade</u>
3 garlic cloves, minced
5 cm (2 in) knob of ginger, grated
1 tablespoon garam masala
1 tablespoon Kashmiri chilli powder
1 teaspoon ground turmeric
1 teaspoon ground coriander
1 teaspoon freshly ground
  black pepper
1 teaspoon sea salt
1 teaspoon kasoori methi (see Note
  on page 33)
250 g (9 oz/1 cup) full-fat Greek-style
  yoghurt

Cook, stirring occasionally, for 10 minutes or until the chicken is
cooked through and the sauce is thick and bubbling.

Add the butter to the pan and stir until melted and the sauce
is glossy. Sprinkle the kasoori methi over the curry and stir to
combine. Taste and season with more salt if necessary.

Garnish the tikka masala with a few coriander sprigs and serve
with warm naan bread.

HOT CHICKEN SATAY STICKS

With a Malaysian Chinese background, it would be a crime for me not to include chicken satay skewers in this book. Threading the chicken onto bamboo skewers can be time consuming, so it's best to prepare them and the hot satay sauce the day before. When your friends arrive, just fire up the barbecue, grill your satay sticks and let the party begin!

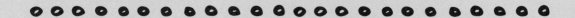

Serves 4–6

500 g (1 lb 2 oz) boneless skinless chicken thighs, sliced into 5 mm x 5 cm (¼ in x 2 in) strips
60 ml (2 fl oz/¼ cup) vegetable oil
1 lemongrass stalk, wide end bashed with the flat side of a knife to make a brush
500 g (1 lb 2 oz/2 cups) Hot satay sauce (see page 154)
1 long cucumber, halved and cut into 1 cm (½ in) thick slices
½ red onion, quartered and layers separated

Marinade
3 lemongrass stalks, white part only, roughly chopped
2.5 cm (1 in) piece of galangal, roughly chopped
3 French shallots
1 tablespoon brown sugar
2 teaspoons ground cumin
2 teaspoons ground coriander
2 teaspoons ground turmeric
2 teaspoons sea salt
60 ml (2 fl oz/¼ cup) vegetable oil

To make the marinade, place all the ingredients in a food processor and process to a fine paste. If the mixture is very thick, add a tablespoon of water and process again.

Pour the marinade into a large bowl, add the chicken and mix until well coated. Cover and transfer to the fridge to marinate for at least 2 hours, but preferably overnight.

Soak about 20 bamboo skewers in water for at least 1 hour. (It is essential that the skewers are damp so they don't catch fire when you put them on the barbecue later.)

Preheat a wood-fired or coal barbecue to medium–high.

Thread 3–4 strips of marinated chicken onto each skewer to cover about two-thirds of the skewer.

Pour the oil into a small bowl and place it next to the barbecue with the lemongrass brush. Working in batches if necessary, grill the chicken skewers on the barbecue, flipping and brushing occasionally with the oil, for 5–6 minutes, until lightly charred on both sides and cooked through.

Serve the chicken skewers with the satay sauce for dipping and a side of cooling cucumber and onion.

GRILLED STEAK WITH CHIMICHURRI

I trust many of you know how to grill steaks to perfection, but please, please, please don't ruin a nice, not to mention expensive, piece of steak by dousing it in gravy made from instant powder mix. The best way to zhoosh up a steak is to pair it with this fresh and herbaceous, yet hot and spicy, dressing known as chimichurri. This Argentinian invention is like liquid gold, as it pairs brilliantly with grilled meat, fish, chicken ... anything really.

Serves 4

4 x 200 g (7 oz) sirloin steaks
sea salt and freshly ground
    black pepper
1 tablespoon olive oil
grilled sweetcorn, fries or steamed
    vegetables, to serve

Chimichurri
15 g ($\frac{1}{2}$ oz/$\frac{3}{4}$ cup) parsley leaves
5 g ($\frac{1}{4}$ oz/$\frac{1}{4}$ cup) coriander (cilantro)
    leaves
3 garlic cloves, roughly chopped
1 red habanero or 2 bird's eye chillies,
    roughly chopped
125 ml (4 fl oz/$\frac{1}{2}$ cup) extra virgin
    olive oil
3 tablespoons red wine vinegar
2 teaspoons fish sauce
$\frac{1}{2}$ teaspoon freshly ground
    black pepper

To make the chimichurri, place the parsley, coriander, garlic, chilli and 2 tablespoons of the olive oil in a blender and blend to a paste. Scrape the mixture into a bowl, add the remaining olive oil along with the vinegar, fish sauce and black pepper and stir to combine. Taste and adjust the seasoning if necessary.

Preheat a barbecue grill to high. Season the steaks generously with salt and pepper and drizzle the olive oil on both sides of the steaks. Once the grill is smoking hot, add the steaks and grill for 3 minutes on each side for medium–rare. Remove the steaks from the grill, transfer to a tray and cover loosely with foil. Set aside to rest for 5 minutes.

Slice the steaks against the grain and drizzle over the chimichurri. Serve with a side of grilled sweetcorn, fries or steamed vegetables for those who are health conscious.

JALAPENO FIRE STARTERS

Let's get the party started with these insanely good fire starters! They're so easy to prepare you can almost make them with your eyes closed (or maybe not). The reward? A mountain of molten meatballs hot enough to numb your lips and keep you coming back for more. Once you pop, you can't stop!

Makes about 20

500 g (1 lb 2 oz) minced (ground) beef
2 jalapeno chillies, finely chopped
1 tablespoon Cajun seasoning
1 teaspoon sea salt
1 teaspoon freshly ground
    black pepper
1 teaspoon smoked paprika
1 teaspoon cayenne pepper
2 teaspoons garlic powder
50 g (1¾ oz/½ cup) dry breadcrumbs
1 free-range egg
125 g (4½ oz) firm mozzarella, cut into
    1 cm (½ in) cubes
vegetable oil, for brushing
250 g (9 oz/1 cup) whole-egg
    mayonnaise
1 tablespoon Sriracha hot sauce
    (see page 158 or use store-bought)

Preheat the oven to 200°C (400°F). Line a baking tray with baking paper.

Place the beef, jalapeno, Cajun seasoning, salt, black pepper, paprika, cayenne pepper, garlic powder, breadcrumbs and egg in a bowl. Use your hands to mix everything together until well combined.

Scoop a tablespoon of the mince mixture into your hand and roll it into a ball, then flatten into a round disc. Place a cube of mozzarella in the centre, fold the mince mixture over the cheese and roll to seal. Place the meatball on the prepared tray, then repeat to make about 20 meatballs.

Brush the meatballs with vegetable oil, then bake in the oven for 10–15 minutes, until cooked through. Set aside to rest for 5 minutes.

Meanwhile, combine the mayonnaise and sriracha in a bowl to make a dipping sauce.

Serve the meatballs with the sriracha mayonnaise, remembering that the cheese inside will be molten hot!

SAMBAL-FRIED BOILED EGGS

Like most kids growing up in Southeast Asia, we were trained to eat spicy food at a very young age. I still remember my mum occasionally preparing these sambal eggs and packing them into my lunchbox, along with some rice and cucumber slices for me to take to school. These eggs also go really well with nasi lemak, the fragrant national rice dish of Malaysia.

Serves 2–4

125 ml (4 fl oz/½ cup) vegetable oil
4 hard-boiled free-range eggs, peeled
1 large onion, thinly sliced
125 g (4½ oz/½ cup) Sambal
   belachan (see page 155)
1 tablespoon tamarind concentrate
1 tablespoon grated palm or
   brown sugar
sea salt
handful of coriander (cilantro) sprigs,
   to garnish
steamed rice, to serve
sliced cucumber, to serve

Heat the vegetable oil in a frying pan over medium heat. Add the eggs and shallow-fry them, tossing occasionally, for 4–6 minutes, until golden brown on all sides. (Make sure the oil isn't too hot or the eggs will explode and hot oil will splatter everywhere!) Using a slotted spoon, remove the eggs from the pan and drain on paper towel. Discard all but 1 tablespoon of the oil in the pan.

Increase the heat to medium–high, add the onion and cook for 1–2 minutes, until soft. Add the sambal belachan, tamarind concentrate, sugar and 125 ml (4 fl oz/½ cup) water, then stir to combine and bring to the boil. Reduce the heat to medium–low and simmer until the sauce has thickened and reduced by half. Taste and season with salt.

Cut the eggs in half and place in serving bowls. Spoon the sambal sauce over the top and garnish with coriander sprigs. Serve warm or at room temperature with steamed rice and sliced cucumber to counteract the heat.

NASHVILLE HOT CHICKEN

It's called 'hot chicken' because it's spicy hot! A local specialty of Nashville, Tennessee, this fried chicken is to die for. I didn't go too crazy with the heat level in this recipe and settled on two tablespoons of cayenne pepper, and I think it's just right. For those who like to play with fire, try six tablespoons and get ready to burn the house down.

Serves 2–4

1.5 kg (3 lb 5 oz) whole chicken, cut
    into 8 pieces
300 g (10½ oz/2 cups) plain
    (all-purpose) flour
140 g (5 oz) rice flour
1 teaspoon garlic powder
1 teaspoon onion powder
2 tablespoons cayenne pepper, plus
    extra to serve
1 tablespoon smoked paprika, plus
    extra to serve
vegetable oil, for shallow-frying
90 g (3 oz/⅓ cup) whole-egg
    mayonnaise
1 tablespoon Sriracha hot sauce
    (see page 158 or use store-bought)
sea salt, to taste

Spicy buttermilk brine
2 tablespoons sea salt
2 tablespoons sugar
1 litre (34 fl oz/4 cups) buttermilk
1 tablespoon cayenne pepper
1 tablespoon smoked paprika
1 tablespoon freshly ground
    black pepper
2 tablespoons hot sauce, such as
    Frank's RedHot or Tapatío

To make the buttermilk brine, place the ingredients in a bowl and whisk until the sugar has dissolved. Pour the mixture into a large zip-lock bag. Add the chicken, then seal and gently massage to coat the chicken in the brine. Set aside in the fridge overnight.

In a large bowl, combine the plain and rice flours, garlic and onion powders, cayenne pepper and smoked paprika and whisk to combine.

Set up a workstation with the chicken in brine in one bowl, the flour mixture and a baking tray. Take a piece of chicken, removing as much of the brine as possible by scraping it on the side of the bowl, then dredge in the flour mixture until fully coated. Shake off the excess flour and place the chicken on the baking tray. Repeat with the remaining chicken.

Once all the chicken is coated, repeat the process to double-coat the chicken, then set aside to rest for 15 minutes.

Heat about 5 cm (2 in) of vegetable oil in a large heavy-based frying pan or flameproof casserole dish over medium–high heat to 160°C (320°F) on a cook's thermometer. Working in batches, fry the chicken, turning occasionally, for 15 minutes or until crispy and golden brown. Always check and make sure you bring the oil back up to temperature before frying the next batch. Using a slotted spoon, remove the chicken and drain on paper towel.

While the chicken drains, quickly combine the mayonnaise and sriracha in a small serving bowl.

Sprinkle extra cayenne pepper, smoked paprika and salt to taste over the chicken and toss to coat. Serve immediately with the sriracha mayonnaise.

KILLER KIMCHI FRIED RICE

This might sound strange, but whenever I am feeling under the weather I like to eat spicy food to sweat it all out. Kimchi fried rice is my saviour; all you need is some left-over cooked rice and spicy fermented kimchi. Give them a quick stir-fry and you'll have delicious fried rice in no time. You'll be sweating bullets before you know it.

Serves 4

200 g (7 oz/1 cup) kimchi
1 tablespoon vegetable oil
550 g (1 lb 3 oz/3 cups) day-old
   cooked jasmine rice
2–3 tablespoons gochujang (see Note)
2 teaspoons soy sauce
1 tablespoon sesame oil
1 spring onion (scallion), thinly sliced
4 fried free-range eggs, to
   serve (optional)
1 tablespoon toasted sesame seeds
1 small nori sheet, cut into thin strips

Squeeze all the juice from the kimchi into a bowl – you need about 60 ml (2 fl oz/¼ cup) of kimchi juice. Finely chop the kimchi and set aside.

Heat the vegetable oil in a wok or large frying pan over medium–high heat. Add the chopped kimchi and stir-fry for 1 minute or until fragrant and slightly charred. Stir through the rice, breaking up the grains with the back of a wooden spoon, then add the kimchi juice, gochujang and soy sauce and stir-fry for 5 minutes or until well combined and fragrant.

Remove the pan from the heat, add the sesame oil and spring onion and give the fried rice a quick stir. Divide the fried rice among serving bowls and top each bowl with a fried egg, if you like. Sprinkle the sesame seeds and nori over the top and serve hot.

Note: Gochujang is a fermented chilli paste widely used in Korean cuisine. It is available from Asian supermarkets.

SPIC
YOUR

SEARING WHOLE ROASTED CAULIFLOWER

The beauty of this recipe is in its simplicity. You don't even have to remove the cauliflower florets! Instead you just roast the whole head. The Indian-inspired spice paste has quite a kick, so serve it with some cooling Greek-style yoghurt on the side.

Serves 4–6

1 head of cauliflower
250 g (9 oz/1 cup) Greek-style yoghurt, plus extra to serve
zest and juice of 1 lime
2 teaspoons chilli powder
1 teaspoon chilli flakes
1 teaspoon all-purpose curry powder
1 tablespoon garlic powder
1 tablespoon ground cumin
2 teaspoons sea salt
1 teaspoon freshly ground black pepper

Place the cauliflower in a large steamer set over a saucepan of simmering water. Steam the cauliflower for 10–15 minutes, until soft but not falling apart. Set the cauliflower aside to cool to room temperature, then trim the base of the cauliflower so it can sit upright.

Preheat the oven to 200°C (400°F). Line a baking tray with baking paper.

Combine the remaining ingredients in a large shallow bowl. Holding the cauliflower by the stalk, dip the cauliflower into the yoghurt mixture, then use your hand to evenly smear the mixture all over the cauliflower. Transfer the cauliflower to the prepared tray and roast for 30–45 minutes, until completely golden brown with a crust on top.

Set the cauliflower aside to cool for 10 minutes before cutting into wedges. Serve with extra Greek-style yoghurt on the side.

SPICY RED LENTIL CURRY SOUP

Every cook should have this recipe in their repertoire. This one-pot wonder is the perfect solution for those winter nights when you just want a big warm bowl of spicy goodness on the couch in front of the TV. Keep any leftovers in the fridge and reheat the next day; the curry soup will be even more flavourful.

Serves 4–6

2 tablespoons vegetable oil

1 large onion, finely chopped

1 large jalapeno or long red chilli, finely chopped

5 cm (2 in) knob of ginger, grated

3 garlic cloves, finely chopped

2 tomatoes, diced

1 teaspoon ground cumin

1 teaspoon ground coriander

1 teaspoon ground turmeric

¼ teaspoon chilli flakes

2 tablespoons Thai red curry paste

40 g (1½ oz) tomato paste (concentrated purée)

375 g (13 oz/1½ cups) red lentils, rinsed and drained

125 ml (4 fl oz/½ cup) coconut milk

sea salt

handful of coriander (cilantro) sprigs, to garnish

steamed rice, to serve (optional)

Heat the oil in a large saucepan over medium–high heat. Add the onion and cook for 2–3 minutes, until soft and translucent. Add the jalapeno or red chilli, ginger, garlic and tomato and cook, stirring, for 1 minute. Add the cumin, ground coriander, turmeric, chilli flakes, curry paste and tomato paste and cook, stirring, for a further 2 minutes. Add 500 ml (17 fl oz/2 cups) water, stir to combine and bring to the boil. Stir through the lentils and coconut milk and season with salt.

Reduce the heat to medium–low, cover and simmer, stirring occasionally, for 15–20 minutes, until the lentils are tender and cooked through. If the curry gets too thick, add a tablespoon of water at a time until you have a nice thick soup consistency. Taste and adjust the seasoning if necessary.

Garnish the curry with coriander sprigs and serve on its own or with steamed rice.

CURRY LAKSA

Curry laksa or laksa lemak is a well-loved Malaysian curry noodle soup that can be eaten for breakfast, lunch or dinner. Many locals believe that eating spicy food in the sweltering heat creates a cooling effect because the food causes you to sweat. So, if there aren't any beads of sweat dripping down your face and chilli oil splatters on your shirt, then you obviously haven't added enough chilli!

Serves 4

200 g (7 oz) dried rice vermicelli
450 g (1 lb) fresh hokkien egg noodles
1 chicken breast fillet
500 g (1 lb 2 oz) raw prawns (shrimp), peeled and deveined, tails left intact (keep the prawn heads and shells to make the stock)
125 ml (4 fl oz/½ cup) vegetable oil
250 g (9 oz/1 cup) Rempah spice paste (see page 156)
400 ml (13½ fl oz) tin coconut cream
sea salt, to taste
200 g (7 oz) fried tofu puffs, halved
200 g (7 oz) bean sprouts
2 hard-boiled free-range eggs, halved
handful of mint leaves
handful of Vietnamese coriander (cilantro) (optional)

Soak the rice vermicelli in warm water for 20 minutes until soft. Drain and set aside.

Meanwhile, place the hokkien noodles in a microwave-safe bowl, then microwave on high for 3 minutes to soften. Using a fork, loosen and separate the noodles. Set aside with the vermicelli noodles, ready to be used.

Fill a large stockpot with 2 litres (68 fl oz/8 cups) water and bring to the boil over high heat. Add the chicken, reduce the heat to medium–low and simmer for 15–20 minutes, until the chicken is cooked through. Using a slotted spoon, remove the chicken and set aside to cool, then slice the chicken into thin pieces.

In the same stockpot, add the prawn heads and shells and bring back to a rolling boil over high heat. Reduce the heat to medium and simmer for 30 minutes to make a prawn stock. Strain the stock into a clean saucepan and discard the solids.

Heat the vegetable oil in a wok or large frying pan over medium heat. Add the rempah spice paste and cook, stirring frequently, for 15–20 minutes, until the oil has split from the paste and the cooked paste is a dark-brown colour.

Add the cooked paste to the prawn stock and stir to combine. Pour in the coconut cream and bring to the boil over medium–high heat. Taste and season with salt. Add the tofu puffs, then reduce the heat to a simmer.

Grab a quarter of the hokkien noodles and rice vermicelli and place inside a wire-mesh strainer. Add a quarter of the prawns and dunk the strainer into the hot laksa broth and let it cook for 1 minute. Lift the strainer out and place the cooked noodles and prawns into a serving bowl. Repeat with the remaining noodles and prawns.

Divide the chicken, bean sprouts and halved hard-boiled eggs evenly among the bowls, then ladle over the hot laksa broth along with the tofu puffs. Garnish with the mint leaves and Vietnamese coriander (if using) and serve immediately.

NUMBING LARB MOO

Isan is a region in northeastern Thailand well known for its super spicy food. Larb moo may look like a simple minced (ground) pork salad, but it is actually a very complex-tasting dish filled with layer upon layer of flavour. You can also make this dish using chicken or beef mince.

Serves 2

100 g (3½ oz/½ cup) glutinous
　　sticky rice
300 g (10½ oz) minced (ground) pork
1 tablespoon ground Thai or Korean
　　chilli flakes
1 tablespoon fish sauce
2 tablespoons freshly squeezed
　　lime juice
3–4 Asian shallots, finely chopped
large handful of coriander
　　(cilantro) leaves, roughly chopped
5–10 Thai scud or bird's eye
　　chillies (depending on how much
　　heat you can take)
steamed jasmine rice, to serve

Heat-relief side plate

1 cos (romaine) or butter lettuce,
　　leaves separated
1 bunch snake (yard-long) or green
　　beans, cut into 5 cm (2 in) lengths
handful of mint leaves
1 bunch Thai coriander (see Note)

Place the sticky rice in a dry wok or large frying pan over medium–low heat. Toast the rice, stirring frequently, for 10–15 minutes, until golden brown and it smells like popcorn. Transfer the toasted rice to a mortar and pestle and grind to a powder.

Bring 125 ml (4 fl oz/½ cup) water to the boil in a saucepan over medium heat. Add the minced pork and cook, stirring, for 3–5 minutes, until the mince is cooked and most of the water has evaporated, leaving about 1 tablespoon of liquid in the pan. Turn off the heat.

While the mince is still warm in the saucepan, add the chilli flakes, fish sauce and lime juice and mix well, then add the shallot and 1 tablespoon of the ground rice, stirring to combine. The sticky rice will help to thicken the sauce, but if it still looks too saucy, add a little more ground rice and stir until it reaches your desired consistency. Add the coriander and whole chillies and mix well.

Serve the larb moo with the lettuce, beans, mint leaves and Thai coriander and, of course, a bowl of steamed jasmine rice on the side.

Note: Thai coriander, also known as Chinese parsley, is an aromatic herb commonly used in Thai and Vietnamese cuisines. You can purchase it at Thai grocers. Ask for 'pak chee'.

ANGRY ARRABBIATA WITH SPICY SAUSAGE

You simply can't go wrong with the combination of fiery arrabbiata sauce and spicy Italian sausage. Arrabbiata means 'angry' in Italian and it refers to the amount of chilli used in this dish. I prefer to use penne as the tube-shaped pasta holds the sauce really well, but feel free to experiment with other types of pasta.

Serves 4

350 g (12½ oz) dried penne
1 tablespoon extra virgin olive oil
250 g (9 oz) spicy Italian sausages
1 large onion, finely chopped
3 garlic cloves, finely chopped
2 bird's eye chillies, finely chopped
500 ml (17 fl oz/2 cups) Arrabbiata sauce (see page 159)
sea salt and freshly ground black pepper
grated parmesan, to serve
finely chopped parsley leaves, to serve (optional)

Bring a large saucepan of salted water to a rolling boil over high heat. Add the penne, reduce the heat to a simmer and cook until al dente. If you're timings are right, the pasta should be ready when the sauce is ready to mingle.

Meanwhile, heat the olive oil in a large deep frying pan over medium heat. Add the sausages and sauté for 5 minutes or until well browned and cooked through. Transfer the sausages to a chopping board and leave to cool slightly, then cut into 1 cm (½ in) thick diagonal slices.

In the same pan, sauté the onion for 2 minutes or until soft and translucent, then add the garlic and chilli and sauté for 2 minutes or until fragrant.

Return the sausage to the pan and stir in the arrabbiata sauce, scraping up any caramelised bits stuck to the base of the pan.

By now, the pasta should be ready. Drain the pasta, reserving 250 ml (8½ fl oz/1 cup) of the pasta cooking water. Add the pasta and half the cooking water to the arrabbiata sauce and stir until combined. If you like your pasta saucy, add more pasta water, a little at a time, until you reach the desired consistency. Taste and season with salt and pepper.

Divide the pasta among serving bowls and top with as little or as much parmesan as you like (you can never have too much cheese in my book!). Sprinkle chopped parsley over the top if you like and serve immediately.

FIRE DUMPLINGS IN CHILLI OIL

Have you ever hosted a dumpling party? I like to invite my friends over and gather around the dinner table, where we banter and fold dumplings together. Then we all share our reward of silky smooth dumplings doused in red-hot chilli oil, washed down with a cold beer. It's absolutely my favourite past-time.

Makes 40–50

40–50 square gyoza wrappers
spring onions (scallions), thinly sliced,
  to garnish

Dumpling filling
500 g (1 lb 2 oz) fatty minced
  (ground) pork
1 bunch garlic chives, finely chopped
1 free-range egg
2 teaspoons sesame oil
1 tablespoon light soy sauce
1 tablespoon Shaoxing rice wine
2 teaspoons ground white pepper
1 tablespoon cornflour (corn starch)

Spicy dumpling sauce (serves 1)
1 tablespoon Sichuan chilli oil
  (see page 157), plus extra to serve
1 tablespoon light soy sauce
1 teaspoon dark soy sauce
2 teaspoons Chinese black rice
  vinegar
pinch of freshly ground black pepper
1 teaspoon pork lard (optional)

To make the dumpling filling, place all the ingredients in a large bowl and use a fork or chopsticks to mix vigorously for 2–3 minutes, until the mixture is homogenous and sticky.

Set up a workstation with a small bowl of water, the dumpling filling, gyoza wrappers and a baking tray lined with baking paper.

Place a wrapper in your palm, then place a teaspoon of filling in the centre. Fold the wrapper in half into a triangle, dab some water on the two longest points, then fold both points round to meet each other and pinch together to seal. The dumpling should look like a mini boat, similar to a tortellini. Place the dumpling on the prepared tray and repeat to make 40–50 dumplings.

Bring a saucepan of water to the boil over medium–high heat. Working in batches of 10 dumplings at a time, carefully lower the dumplings into the pan and give the water a quick stir. Reduce the heat to a simmer and cook the dumplings, stirring occasionally, for 3–5 minutes, until they float to the surface.

To make the spicy dumpling sauce, place all the ingredients in a serving bowl. Ladle 60 ml (2 fl oz/¼ cup) of the boiling dumpling water into the bowl and stir to combine. Repeat this process to make portions of dumpling sauce for each of your guests.

Once the dumplings are ready, scoop them out using a wire-mesh strainer or slotted spoon and transfer to the bowls with the spicy dumpling sauce. Drizzle extra chilli oil over the dumplings and garnish with spring onion.

GONG BAO CHICKEN

I always thought gong bao chicken was relatively mild; that is until I had the real deal in Sichuan province in China. That's when I first truly experienced the numbing effect from the insane amount of Sichuan peppercorns used in this dish. If you are allergic to peanuts, just leave them out.

Serves 2

300 g (10½ oz) boneless skinless
   chicken thighs, cut into 2 cm
   (¾ in) pieces
vegetable oil, for frying
5 dried chillies, cut into 2 cm
   (¾ in) lengths
2 teaspoons Sichuan peppercorns
2.5 cm (1 in) knob of ginger, grated
2 garlic cloves, thinly sliced
30 g (1 oz) unsalted roasted peanuts
3 spring onions (scallions), cut into
   1 cm (½ in) lengths

Gong bao sauce
1½ tablespoons Shaoxing rice wine
2 teaspoons light soy sauce
1 teaspoon dark soy sauce
2 teaspoons Chinese black
   rice vinegar
1 teaspoon ground white pepper
1 tablespoon sugar
1 teaspoon cornflour (corn starch)

Chicken marinade
½ teaspoon sea salt
½ teaspoon ground white pepper
1 tablespoon Shaoxing rice wine
1 teaspoon dark soy sauce
2 teaspoons cornflour (corn starch)
1 tablespoon vegetable oil

To marinate the chicken, combine the marinade ingredients except the vegetable oil in a large bowl. Add the chicken and mix well to completely coat the chicken. Stir in the vegetable oil and set aside for at least 5 minutes.

To make the gong bao sauce, combine the ingredients in a bowl and set aside.

Heat 500 ml (17 fl oz/2 cups) of vegetable oil in a wok or large frying pan over high heat. Once smoking, turn off the heat and add the chicken. Flash-fry the chicken for 1 minute or until seared all over. Using a slotted spoon, transfer the chicken to a heatproof bowl lined with paper towel. Drain all but 2 tablespoons of the oil.

Heat the remaining oil in the wok or pan over medium–high heat. Add the chilli and Sichuan peppercorns and stir-fry for 10 seconds. Add the ginger and garlic and stir-fry for 1 minute or until fragrant. Return the chicken to the wok or pan and stir-fry for 1 minute to infuse in the oil. Pour in the gong bao sauce, increase the heat to high and stir-fry for 1–2 minutes or until the sauce thickens and the chicken is cooked through. Add the peanuts and spring onion, give everything a quick stir, then transfer to a serving plate and serve immediately.

SALMON NIGIRI SUSHI ROULETTE

Just as lethal as playing Russian roulette, but with wasabi! The rule is simple: invite your friends to select a piece of sushi and eat it in one go. There's nothing more cruel (hilarious) than waiting for someone to swallow a large lump of wasabi, and then choke and cry in agony. I advise you to play this game with close friends only!

Makes 10

150 g (5½ oz) sushi-grade salmon
wasabi paste, to taste
sushi pickled ginger, to serve
sushi soy sauce, to serve

Sushi rice
220 g (8 oz/1 cup) sushi rice
3 teaspoons sushi rice vinegar
1 teaspoon sea salt
2½ teaspoons sugar

To make the sushi rice, rinse the rice in a bowl of cold water, then drain. Repeat this process three to five times, until the water turns from murky to almost clear. You can cook the rice in a rice cooker or place in a saucepan with 375 ml (12½ fl oz/1½ cups) water and bring to the boil over medium–high heat. Give the rice a stir to make sure it doesn't stick to the bottom of the pan, then reduce the heat to low, cover and simmer for 20 minutes or until the rice has absorbed the water and is cooked through.

Carefully spread the hot rice on a tray or large platter. Combine the vinegar, salt and sugar in a jug and stir until dissolved. Pour the vinegar mixture evenly over the rice, then use a spatula to fold the rice a few times to incorporate the vinegar mixture. Set aside to cool to room temperature.

Meanwhile, prepare the salmon. Using a very sharp knife, carefully slice the salmon on an angle into ten 5 mm (¼ in) thick strips.

Set up a workstation of sushi rice, salmon and wasabi paste. Wet your hands so the rice doesn't stick, then place a tablespoon of rice in your palm and press firmly using the index and middle fingers of your other hand to shape the rice into a small rectangular pillow. Dab a small amount of wasabi paste on top of the rice, then drape over a slice of salmon to seal. Repeat the process with the remaining rice, salmon and wasabi, but place a big dollop of wasabi on one of the nigiri.

Arrange the salmon nigiri in a circle on a platter and serve with pickled ginger and soy sauce on the side.

Let the sushi roulette begin!

SCORCHING SOM TAM

Som tam is a much-loved street-food dish from Thailand. On the one hand, it's cool and refreshing with the fresh crunch of tangy green papaya. On the other hand, it often contains so much chilli you'll be thankful for that cold Chang beer you just ordered. Of course, you can reduce the amount of chilli you add, but where's the fun in that?

Serves 4

2 large garlic cloves, roughly chopped

3–5 bird's eye chillies (depending on how hot you like it), roughly chopped

1½ tablespoons grated palm sugar

2 tablespoons dried shrimp, soaked in hot water for 20 minutes, drained

30 g (1 oz) unsalted peanuts, toasted, roughly chopped

5 snake (yard-long) beans, cut into 2.5 cm (1 in) lengths

200 g (7 oz) cherry tomatoes, halved

1 green papaya, shredded

3 tablespoons fish sauce, plus extra if needed

3 tablespoons freshly squeezed lime juice, plus extra if needed

roughly chopped coriander (cilantro) leaves, to serve

In a large mortar and pestle, pound the garlic, chillies and sugar to a paste. Add the rehydrated shrimp and half the peanuts and pound again, then add the snake beans and cherry tomatoes and gently crush. Transfer to a large bowl.

Toss the green papaya through the snake bean mixture, then stir through the fish sauce and lime juice. Taste the salad – the flavour should be salty, sour, sweet and hot – and add more fish sauce and lime juice if necessary.

Transfer the som tam to a serving bowl, top with the remaining peanuts and the coriander and serve.

THE HOT KFC

I love all kinds of fried chicken, but Korean fried chicken is my ultimate kryptonite. It has a lighter flour coating, which gives the chicken a non-greasy crispy skin that still has a crunch to it. It's then coated in that yangnyeom sweet and spicy sauce for orgasmic finger-licking satisfaction.

Serves 4–6

1.5 kg (3 lb 5 oz) chicken wings
1 teaspoon sea salt
1 teaspoon freshly ground
    black pepper
1 cm (½ in) knob of ginger, minced
90 g (3 oz/½ cup) potato starch
45 g (1½ oz/¼ cup) rice flour
35 g (1¼ oz/¼ cup) plain
    (all-purpose) flour
1 teaspoon bicarbonate of
    soda (baking soda)
1 free-range egg
vegetable oil, for shallow-frying
toasted sesame seeds, to garnish
steamed rice, to serve

Yangnyeom sauce
1 tablespoon vegetable oil
4 garlic cloves, finely chopped
2 tablespoons soy sauce
2 tablespoons gochujang (see Note
    on page 67)
1 tablespoon white vinegar
1 tablespoon Korean rice
    syrup (ssalyeot; see Note on
    page 98) or corn syrup
2 tablespoons sugar

Cut the chicken wings into three: the meaty drumette, the wingette and the tip. Discard the tips or reserve them to make chicken stock. Place the chicken in a large bowl, along with the salt, pepper and ginger and rub into the chicken. Add the potato starch, rice flour, plain flour, bicarbonate of soda and egg. Toss everything together until the chicken is thickly coated in the flour mixture.

Heat about 5 cm (2 in) of vegetable oil in a large heavy-based saucepan or flameproof casserole dish until it reaches 165°C (330°F) on a cook's thermometer. Working in batches, fry the chicken pieces, turning occasionally to prevent them sticking together, for 10–12 minutes, until light golden brown. Using tongs, remove the chicken and transfer to a wire rack with paper towel underneath to catch the excess oil.

Bring the oil temperature back to 165°C (330°F). Working in batches, fry the chicken pieces a second time for 12–15 minutes, until they are deep golden brown and super crunchy. Remove and transfer back to the wire rack to drain.

While the chicken is frying, make the yangnyeom sauce. Heat the oil in a large non-stick frying pan or wok over medium–high heat. Add the garlic and stir-fry for 1 minute until fragrant. Add the remaining ingredients and stir until the sugar has dissolved. Reduce the heat to medium and simmer for 2–3 minutes, or until the sauce has thickened and reduced by half.

Add the fried chicken to the pan and give it a quick toss to coat the chicken in the sauce. Transfer to a serving plate, sprinkle with sesame seeds and serve immediately with steamed rice.

FLAMIN' TACOS

These are not your typical tacos but a fusion of East meets West, a happy marriage of two of my favourite cuisines — Mexican and Korean. The sweetness of the bulgogi beef works exceptionally well with the flamin' chilli mayo. My advice to you is to go easy on the Korean capsaicin hot sauce, as a little goes a long way. You've been warned!

Makes 8

vegetable oil, for greasing
8 soft corn tortillas, warmed
200 g (7 oz/1 cup) kimchi, chopped
1 large red onion, finely diced
1 bunch coriander (cilantro), leaves
    roughly chopped
lime wedges, to serve

Flamin' chilli mayo

250 g (9 oz/1 cup) mayonnaise
2 tablespoons kimchi juice
2 tablespoons gochujang
1 teaspoon Korean capsaicin hot
    sauce (see Note)
2 teaspoons rice vinegar
3 garlic cloves, minced
2.5 cm (1 in) knob of ginger, grated
2 teaspoons sesame oil
1 tablespoon caster (superfine) sugar

Bulgogi beef

600 g (1 lb 5 oz) rib-eye or sirloin steak
5 garlic cloves, finely chopped
2 tablespoons light soy sauce
2 tablespoons light brown sugar
1 tablespoon sesame oil
1 tablespoon gochujang (see Note
    on page 67)
5 cm (2 in) knob of ginger, grated
5 garlic cloves, minced
1 large onion, thinly sliced

To make the bulgogi beef, wrap the steak in plastic wrap and freeze for 30 minutes to firm up. Unwrap the steak and thinly slice it against the grain. Place the steak and remaining bulgogi ingredients in a bowl, mix well to coat the steak, then cover and set aside in the fridge to marinate for at least 2 hours, but preferably overnight.

To make the chilli mayo, place all the ingredients in a blender and pulse a few times until well blended. Pour the chilli mayo into a squeeze bottle if you have one or set aside in a small bowl.

Preheat a barbecue grill plate to high and grease the plate with vegetable oil. Working in batches, cook the steak for 5 minutes or until charred and cooked through. Transfer to a bowl and set aside.

To assemble the tacos, place the tortillas on a chopping board and evenly divide the bulgogi beef among them. Add a spoonful of kimchi and squeeze some chilli mayo over the top. Garnish with onion, coriander and lime wedges, and devour.

Note: Korean capsaicin is a spice enhancer with a Scoville Heat Scale of over 15,000,000! So you only need a little to feel the burn. It can be purchased from any Korean supermarket.

HOT SAUCE BUFFALO WINGS

An American classic, these spicy hot buffalo wings are the perfect party food for when your mates come round for game night. Instead of deep-frying the wings, I find baking them actually yields juicier wings that are more fall-off-the-bone tender. If you want the wings to be extra crispy, try adding baking powder following the method on page 36 for the Sriracha and honey chicken wings before baking.

Serves 4

1 kg (2 lb 3 oz) chicken wingettes
    and drumettes
2 teaspoons sea salt
1 teaspoon freshly ground
    black pepper
3 celery stalks, cut into batons
1 large carrot, cut into batons

Buffalo hot sauce
125 ml (4 fl oz/½ cup) Sriracha hot
    sauce (see page 158 or use
    store-bought)
1 teaspoon cayenne pepper
1 teaspoon chilli powder
2 teaspoons smoked paprika
1 teaspoon Worcestershire sauce
125 g (4½ oz) cold butter, cut into
    1 cm (½ in) cubes

Blue cheese dipping sauce
150 g (5½ oz) blue cheese, such
    as Stilton
250 g (9 oz/1 cup) sour cream
juice of ½ lemon
1 tablespoon white vinegar
sea salt and freshly ground
    black pepper

To make the buffalo hot sauce, place the sriracha, cayenne pepper, chilli powder, smoked paprika and Worcestershire sauce in a saucepan over medium heat and bring to a simmer. Whisk in the cold butter gradually, two or three cubes at a time, until fully incorporated and the sauce looks glossy. Remove from the heat and set aside to cool completely.

Place the chicken in a large bowl with the salt, pepper and 60 ml (2 fl oz/¼ cup) of the hot sauce. Mix everything together until the chicken is nicely coated, then set aside in the fridge to marinate for at least 1 hour, but preferably overnight.

Preheat the oven to 200°C (400°F). Place the chicken pieces on a wire rack in a single layer with space between them. Bake in the oven for 1 hour, turning the chicken halfway through cooking, until golden brown and crispy.

When the chicken is almost done, make the dipping sauce. Use a fork to mash the cheese to a paste (small lumps are okay), then whisk in the sour cream, lemon juice and vinegar. Taste and season with salt and pepper.

Transfer the chicken to a bowl, add the remaining hot sauce and toss until the chicken is nicely coated. Serve immediately with the blue cheese dipping sauce and celery and carrot on the side for a refreshing crunch.

PIRI-PIRI CHICKEN

While many of us know and love piri-piri chicken as a Portuguese dish, you may not know that the piri-piri chilli itself has roots in Angola and Mozambique. In Swahili, piri (or pili) means 'pepper' and because the chilli is so hot, they have to name it twice, hence the name. The piri-piri sauce in this dish goes really well with seafood, too!

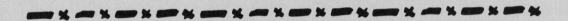

Serves 4

1.5 kg (3 lb 5 oz) whole chicken
potato chips (crisps) and slaw
   of your choice, to serve

Piri-piri sauce
4 garlic cloves, roughly chopped
2 French shallots, roughly chopped
juice of 1 lemon
5 long red chillies, roughly chopped
2.5 cm (1 in) knob of ginger, roughly
   chopped
1 tablespoon red wine vinegar
100 ml (3½ fl oz) extra virgin olive oil
1 teaspoon smoked paprika
½ teaspoon cayenne pepper
2 teaspoons sea salt
1 teaspoon freshly ground
   black pepper

Preheat the oven to 200°C (400°F).

To make the piri-piri sauce, blitz the ingredients in a food processor to a loose paste. Transfer the paste to a heavy-based frying pan over medium heat and cook, stirring frequently, for 10 minutes or until browned. Transfer the paste to a heatproof jug and set aside to cool completely.

To butterfly the chicken, place the chicken on a chopping board, breast side down. Using a pair of kitchen scissors and starting at the base, cut along each side of the spine and remove the backbone. Flip the chicken over, breast side up, place the palm of your hand in the middle of the breast bone and press down firmly to crack the bone and flatten the chicken.

Brush the chicken all over with some of the piri-piri sauce, then transfer to a roasting tin and bake in the oven, basting the chicken with extra piri-piri sauce every 15 minutes, for 45 minutes or until the chicken is cooked through.

Meanwhile, preheat a barbecue grill plate to hot.

Brush the cooked chicken with the piri-piri sauce one last time, then place on the hot barbecue and grill for 3 minutes or until slightly charred all over.

Transfer the chicken to a chopping board and cut it into pieces. Slather extra piri-piri sauce over the chicken and serve with potato chips and slaw on the side.

SPICY KOREAN BARBECUE PORK

Koreans have a strong love affair with spicy food and this dish is a classic example, which everyone should learn how to make. It is especially popular with office workers and uni students not only because it's super tasty, but it's also cheap and readily available. Korean barbecue pork usually scores high on the chilli scale, so by cooking it yourself you can adjust the heat level according to your own taste buds.

Serves 4–6

1 kg (2 lb 3 oz) boneless pork shoulder
1 onion, thinly sliced
3 spring onions (scallions), cut into
   5 cm (2 in) lengths
vegetable oil, for greasing
steamed jasmine rice or cos
   (romaine) lettuce leaves, to serve

Chilli marinade
135 g (5 oz/½ cup) gochujang (see
   Note on page 67)
2 tablespoons gochugaru (see Note)
60 ml (2 fl oz/¼ cup) soy sauce
2 tablespoons rice (or white) vinegar
2 tablespoons sugar
1 tablespoon Korean rice syrup
   (ssalyeot; see Note) or corn syrup
2 tablespoons sesame oil
5 garlic cloves, finely chopped
5 cm (2 in) knob of ginger, finely grated

Freeze the pork for about 1 hour to allow it to firm up, then thinly slice the pork against the grain into 3 mm (⅛ in) thick strips. Combine the pork, onion and spring onion in a large bowl and set aside.

To make the chilli marinade, combine the ingredients in a bowl and stir until the sugar has dissolved. Pour the marinade over the pork and, using your hands (wearing kitchen gloves if you don't want to look like you've committed murder), rub the marinade into the meat until it is well coated. Cover with plastic wrap and set aside to marinate in the fridge for at least 1 hour.

Preheat a barbecue grill plate to high and grease the plate with vegetable oil. Working in batches, cook the pork mixture for 4–5 minutes, until charred and cooked through. Transfer to a bowl and set aside.

Serve the barbecue pork with steamed jasmine rice or cos lettuce leaves on the side to provide a relief from the heat.

Note: Gochugaru is coarsely ground Korean chilli, traditionally used to make kimchi. Ssalyeot is regularly used in Korean cuisine as a sweetener and to add shine to dishes. You can purchase both ingredients at any Korean supermarket.

HELL-RAISING HARISSA CHICKEN

Sunday roast but with a twist! This harissa chicken wins hands down over traditional roast chicken. The harissa takes the flavour of the chicken to the next level, as well as adding a good amount of heat, which, of course, I have increased even further by adding fresh chilli on top. Not to mention, this dish is super easy to put together. Winner winner, chicken dinner.

Serves 4

1.5 kg (3 lb 5 oz) whole chicken, cut into 10 pieces
2 tablespoons olive oil
1 large red chilli, thinly sliced diagonally
1 lime, cut into wedges

Harissa marinade
200 g (7 oz/1 cup) Harissa (see page 161), plus extra to serve
3 garlic cloves, crushed
1 teaspoon sea salt
1 teaspoon freshly ground black pepper
3 tablespoons honey
juice of 1 lime
1 tablespoon olive oil

Place the chicken and all the marinade ingredients in a large bowl. Wearing kitchen gloves, rub the marinade into the chicken until well coated. Set aside in the fridge to marinate for at least 1 hour, but preferably overnight.

Preheat the oven to 190ºC (375ºF).

Heat the olive oil in a large frying pan over medium–high heat. Working in batches, sear the chicken for 3 minutes on each side or until lightly browned. Transfer the chicken to a roasting tin and bake in the oven for 40–45 minutes, until golden brown and slightly charred.

Transfer the chicken to a serving plate and garnish with the chilli. Drizzle a little extra harissa over the top and serve with lime wedges on the side.

CAJUN SHRIMP BOIL

Shrimp boil is not just a recipe, it is a dish that brings people together. Seafood (shrimp, crab and crawfish) boil is a Louisiana Cajun tradition usually prepared for weekend get-togethers or during the holidays when people gather round for a feast. So when you make a shrimp boil, you don't do a half-ass version that only feeds one or two people; instead, you make enough to feed the whole darn neighbourhood. There's something pretty special about seeing everyone peeling shrimp with their fingers and digging in with gusto.

Serves 8

1 large onion, halved
1 lemon, halved
1 kg (2 lb 3 oz) baby (chat) potatoes
2 smoked sausages, such as Kielbasa, andouille or chorizo, thinly sliced diagonally
2 sweetcorn cobs, cut into 3 cm (1¼ in) chunks
2.5 kg (5½ lb) raw prawns (shrimp), peeled and deveined, tails left intact

Shrimp boil seasoning
300 g (10½ oz) butter
1 garlic bulb, cloves finely chopped
2 tablespoons Old Bay Seasoning
2 tablespoons cayenne pepper
2 tablespoons lemon pepper
2 tablespoons smoked paprika
2 tablespoons hot sauce, such as Tapatío or Frank's RedHot
2 tablespoons sugar

To make the shrimp boil seasoning, melt the butter in a large saucepan over medium heat. Add the garlic and sauté for 5 minutes or until fragrant. Add the Old Bay Seasoning, cayenne pepper, lemon pepper and paprika, then stir and cook for 1 minute. Add the hot sauce and sugar and stir until the sugar has dissolved. Reduce the heat to very low and keep warm while you prepare the shrimp boil.

Fill a large stockpot with 8 litres (8½ qts) water. Add the onion and squeeze in the juice from the lemon halves before dropping the halves into the pot, along with 125 ml (4 fl oz/½ cup) of the shrimp boil seasoning. Cover and bring to a rolling boil over medium–high heat. Once boiling, add the potatoes, sausage and corn and boil for 10 minutes or until the potatoes can be easily pierced with a fork but still hold their shape. Add the prawns and bring back to the boil, then cover and boil for 2 minutes.

Using a slotted spoon or wire-mesh strainer, scoop the ingredients out of the pot and transfer to a large mixing bowl. Add 250 ml (8½ fl oz/1 cup) of the stock and the remaining shrimp boil seasoning to the bowl, and stir everything together until well coated. Spoon onto a large platter and ask everyone to dig in with gusto!

Note: You can keep boiling more prawns using the left-over stock; otherwise discard it.

MOLTEN MALAYSIAN CHICKEN CURRY

I might be biased, but my mum's Malaysian chicken curry is world class, not least because she used to set aside a whole day to make it. She would go to the market in the morning to source all the ingredients, then pound the rempah spice paste using a mortar and pestle, and this was all before she even started cooking! Don't worry, my version is a lot simpler and tastes just as good, even if I do say so myself. Sorry Mum!

Serves 4

1.5 kg (3 lb 5 oz) whole chicken, cut into 16 pieces
260 g (9 oz) Rempah spice paste (see page 156)
2 teaspoons sea salt
60 ml (2 fl oz/¼ cup) vegetable oil
a few sprigs of curry leaves, leaves picked
2 star anise
400 ml (13½ fl oz) tin coconut milk
300 g (10½ oz) baby (chat) potatoes, peeled and halved
1 tablespoon sugar
warm roti canai, to serve

Place the chicken, 2 tablespoons of the spice paste and the salt in a large bowl. Using your hands, massage the spice paste and salt into the chicken until nicely coated. Set aside in the fridge to marinate for at least 1 hour, but preferably overnight.

Heat the vegetable oil in a wok or large frying pan over medium heat. Add the remaining spice paste and cook, stirring frequently, for 10–15 minutes, until the oil has separated and the paste is dark brown in colour.

Add the marinated chicken and sear on all sides for 5 minutes. Add the curry leaves and star anise, then pour in the coconut milk and stir to combine. Reduce the heat to medium–low, cover and cook for 20 minutes.

Add the potatoes to the wok or pan, reduce the heat to low and simmer, uncovered and stirring occasionally, for 30–40 minutes, until the chicken is cooked through, the potatoes are tender and the sauce has thickened. Season with salt and the sugar, to taste.

Serve with warm roti canai on the side.

SUPER-CHILLI CON CARNE

Chilli con carne literally means 'chilli with meat', and it doesn't get any simpler than that. There is really no right or wrong way to cook chilli con carne, and anyone you ask will have their own version of the dish. I like to think that my method is possibly the simplest and with very little clean up. Just whack the whole pot in the oven and let it do its job. Chilli con carne is actually quite versatile: serve it with rice, make a burrito or stir it through pasta — the possibilities are endless.

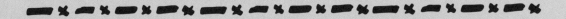

Serves 8

150 g (5½ oz/1 cup) plain
   (all-purpose) flour
1 teaspoon sea salt
1 teaspoon freshly ground
   black pepper
1.5 kg (3 lb 5 oz) beef brisket, cut into
   4 cm (1½ in) chunks
80 ml (2½ fl oz/⅓ cup) olive oil
1 large onion, finely diced
5 garlic cloves, finely chopped
1 teaspoon chilli flakes
½ teaspoon cayenne pepper
40 g (1½ oz) tomato paste
   (concentrated purée)
400 g (14 oz) tin diced or crushed
   tomatoes
230 g (8 oz) chipotles in adobo sauce
500 ml (17 fl oz/2 cups) beef stock
handful of parsley leaves, finely
   chopped (optional)
steamed rice mixed with tinned
   black beans, to serve

Preheat the oven to 160ºC (320ºF).

Combine the flour, salt and pepper in a large bowl. Dredge the beef in the flour, then shake off any excess flour and place the beef on a tray.

Heat half the olive oil in a large frying pan over medium–high heat. Place half the beef in the pan and cook for 5 minutes or until browned on all sides. Transfer the beef to a heavy-based flameproof casserole dish. Add another tablespoon of oil to the pan, cook the remaining beef and also add to the casserole dish.

Heat the remaining oil in the same pan over medium heat. Add the onion and garlic and sauté for 5 minutes or until the onion is soft and translucent. Add the chilli flakes, cayenne pepper and tomato paste and cook for 1 minute. Add the tomatoes, chipotles in adobo sauce and stir well to combine, scraping up any caramelised bits stuck to the base of the pan.

Add the tomato mixture to the casserole dish with the beef, followed by the beef stock. Stir to combine, then bring to the boil over medium–high heat.

Cover and transfer the dish to the oven and cook, stirring once, for 3 hours. Remove the lid and cook for a further 1 hour. Taste and adjust the seasoning if necessary.

Garnish the chilli con carne with parsley (if using) and serve with steamed rice mixed with black beans on the side.

BEEF MADRAS

Not too mild and not too hot, Madras curry is absolutely perfect on a balmy evening. You need a little patience to make this recipe, but slow-cooking the beef will bring out that rich, comforting flavour, with tender meat that requires very little effort. It's totally worth the wait.

Serves 4

1 kg (2 lb 3 oz) gravy or chuck steaks
1 tablespoon sea salt
1 tablespoon olive oil
1 teaspoon black mustard seeds
15 curry leaves
1 large onion, finely diced
5 cm (2 in) knob of ginger, grated
5 garlic cloves, finely chopped
2 long red chillies, finely chopped
400 g (14 oz) tin diced tomatoes
40 g (1½ oz) tomato paste
    (concentrated purée)
1 teaspoon tamarind paste (optional)
steamed basmati rice, to serve

Madras spice mix
2 tablespoons coriander seeds
2 teaspoons fenugreek seeds
1 teaspoon mustard seeds
1 teaspoon cumin seeds
1 teaspoon black peppercorns
1 teaspoon fennel seeds
1 cassia bark, broken into small shards
5 cloves
1 tablespoon ground turmeric
2 teaspoons chilli powder

To make the Madras spice mix, place all the ingredients except the turmeric and chilli powder in a coffee grinder or mortar and pestle and grind to a fine powder. Tip into a bowl and stir through the turmeric and chilli powder.

Cut the beef into 5 cm (2 in) chunks and place in a large bowl with the salt and 2 tablespoons of the Madras spice mix. Using both hands, rub the spice mix and salt into the beef until well coated, then set aside in the fridge to marinate for at least 1 hour. Place the left-over Madras spice mix in a jar and keep it in the pantry for your next curry.

Heat the olive oil in a flameproof casserole dish over medium heat and add the mustard seeds. Once the seeds start to pop and sizzle, add the curry leaves and onion and sauté for 10 minutes or until the onion is caramelised and golden. Add the ginger, garlic and chilli and cook, stirring frequently, for 5 minutes or until the ginger and garlic are caramelised. Add the tomatoes, tomato paste and tamarind paste (if using), then stir and cook for 3 minutes or until the sauce has reduced slightly.

Add the beef to the dish and stir until well coated. Add 250 ml (8½ fl oz/1 cup) water, then reduce the heat to very low, cover and cook, stirring occasionally, for 1½–2 hours, until the beef is cooked through and the sauce has reduced to a thick stew.

Serve the beef Madras with steamed basmati rice.

This dish tastes even better the next day!

XINJIANG LAMB SKEWERS

On the streets of Beijing, you'll find many street-food vendors grilling these lamb skewers over charcoal. The smoky aromas lure you in and before you know it you're chowing down on these fiery morsels of meaty goodness, and, believe me, you can't stop at one. What's even better is that now you can make them at home with this awesome recipe!

Makes 8

1 kg (2 lb 3 oz) boneless lamb
  shoulder (75% lean, 25% fat), lean
  meat cut into 2 cm (¾ in) chunks, fat
  cut into 1 cm (½ in) thick cubes
1 onion, thinly sliced

Dusting spice mix
1 tablespoon ground cumin
2 teaspoons ground Sichuan
  peppercorns
1 tablespoon chilli powder
1 tablespoon toasted sesame seeds

Xinjiang marinade
2 teaspoons ground ginger
2 teaspoons ground Sichuan
  peppercorns
2 teaspoons Chinese five spice
  powder
1 tablespoon ground cumin
2 tablespoons light soy sauce
1 tablespoon Shaoxing rice wine
1 tablespoon chilli powder

Place the lamb, onion and all the marinade ingredients in a large bowl. Using both hands, massage the marinade ingredients into the lamb and onion until completely coated. Cover and set aside to marinate for at least 20 minutes.

Meanwhile, prepare a charcoal barbecue.

Thread the lamb onto eight metal skewers, alternating between two pieces of lean meat and one fat cube. Place the skewers on a tray.

To make the dusting spice mix, combine the ingredients in an empty spice shaker or small bowl, ready to be used.

When the charcoal barbecue has died down with no visible flames and the coals are covered in white ash, it is ready for grilling.

Place the lamb skewers onto the grill spaced evenly apart and cook, turning frequently, for 5–8 minutes, until cooked through and lightly charred all over. Remove the skewers from the grill and dust liberally with the dusting spice mix. Return the skewers to the grill and cook for 10 seconds on both sides. Transfer to a serving plate and consume immediately.

DEATH BY BURRITO

These Korean-twist burritos are seriously tasty, but they also pack a deadly heat punch. When your eyes start to water, your nose runs and your lips curl with a burning sensation, you know you've reached maximum spice levels. Pass me the milk!

Makes 2

vegetable oil, for greasing
2 large flour tortillas
100 g (3½ oz) left-over cooked white
    rice, warmed through
a few cos (romaine) lettuce leaves,
    thinly sliced
100 g (3½ oz/½ cup) kimchi, roughly
    chopped
50 g (1¾ oz/½ cup) shredded cheddar
1 jalapeno chilli, thinly sliced

Soy-marinated barbecue beef
300 g (10½ oz) beef tenderloin or rib-
    eye, thinly sliced against the grain
½ onion, thinly sliced
3 garlic cloves, minced
1 tablespoon caster (superfine) sugar
2 tablespoons soy sauce
1 tablespoon mirin
2 teaspoons sesame oil
½ teaspoon freshly ground
    black pepper

To make the soy-marinated barbecue beef, place all the ingredients in a large bowl and mix well to combine. Set aside in the fridge to marinate for at least 1 hour.

To make the hot sauce dressing, combine the ingredients in a bowl and stir until the sugar has dissolved.

Preheat a barbecue flat plate to high and lightly grease the plate with oil.

Grill the marinated beef for 3 minutes or until cooked and well browned. If you like, use a metal spatula to chop the beef into smaller pieces while cooking. Transfer the cooked beef to a plate, ready to be used.

Briefly warm the tortillas in a dry frying pan over medium heat, flipping for a few seconds on each side until soft and warmed through.

Place the warmed tortillas on a chopping board and spoon the rice evenly down the centre of each tortilla. Top with the lettuce and drizzle over some of the hot sauce dressing, then add the beef, kimchi, cheddar and jalapeno. Drizzle with more hot sauce dressing.

Hot sauce dressing
1 tablespoon vegetable oil
2 tablespoons soy sauce
2 tablespoons gochujang (see Note
  on page 67)
2 teaspoons white vinegar
1 tablespoon caster (superfine) sugar
2 teaspoons Chungwoo capsaicin
  hot sauce (see Note)

Fold in the ends of each tortilla, then roll up tightly into a burrito.
Wrap foil around the bottom half of each burrito to contain any
mess and dig in.

Note: Chungwoo capsaicin hot sauce is Korea's spiciest hot sauce. It is available
online and from Korean supermarkets.

DEVIL'S CURRY
(KARI DEBAL)

When the Portuguese brought chillies to Southeast Asia, a fusion of fiery hot Eurasian 'Peranakan' cuisine was born. 'Kari debal', more commonly known as devil's curry, is one of the most popular, if not hottest, dish in their repertoire. 'Debal' means leftovers in Creole–Portugese, so this dish is usually prepared with cheap ingredients or leftovers from Christmas Day. It's even better the next day once all the ingredients have had a chance to become infused in the hot curry sauce.

Serves 4

1.5 kg (3 lb 5 oz) whole chicken, cut
   into 16 bite-sized pieces
2 tablespoons Worcestershire sauce
1 tablespoon freshly squeezed
   lime juice
3 tablespoons sugar
3 teaspoons sea salt
1 teaspoon ground white pepper
125 ml (4 fl oz/½ cup) vegetable oil
1 red onion, quartered
2 long red chillies, thinly sliced
   diagonally
5 cm (2 in) knob of ginger, grated
125 ml (4 fl oz/½ cup) white vinegar
200 g (7 oz) white cabbage, cut
   into chunks
100 g (3½ oz) cherry tomatoes
steamed jasmine rice or sliced French
   baguette, to serve

Devil's spice paste
30 g (1 oz) dried red chillies, deseeded
   and soaked in hot water for
   30 minutes, drained
100 g (3½ oz) French shallots, roughly
   chopped
2.5 cm (1 in) piece fresh turmeric,
   roughly chopped
5 garlic cloves, roughly chopped

Place the chicken in a large non-reactive dish. Add the Worcestershire sauce, lime juice, 1 tablespoon of the sugar, 1 teaspoon of the salt and the white pepper, then use your hands to massage the ingredients into the chicken until well coated. Set aside in the fridge to marinate for 30 minutes.

To make the spice paste, place the ingredients in a blender and blitz to a fine paste.

Heat the oil in a wok or large frying pan over medium–high heat. Working in batches, sear the chicken for 10 minutes or until browned on all sides. Remove the chicken from the pan and drain on paper towel.

Reheat the vegetable oil in the wok or pan over medium heat, add the spice paste and cook for 10 minutes until the spice paste is a deep red colour and a layer of oil has separated from the spices. Tip the chicken back into the wok or pan, add the onion, chilli and ginger and stir until well coated. Add the vinegar, remaining sugar and salt and stir through 750 ml (25½ fl oz/3 cups) water. Bring to the boil, then reduce the heat to medium–low and simmer for 15 minutes or until the chicken is cooked through and the sauce has reduced by half. Add the cabbage and tomatoes and simmer, stirring occasionally, for 5 minutes.

Serve with steamed jasmine rice or sliced French baguette.

TOM YUM GOONG

You haven't really experienced a true spicy Thai dish until you've eaten tom yum goong. This extremely hot and sour soup is one of the signature dishes that defines Thai flavours. If you want a milder version, you can adjust the heat level by reducing the amount of Thai chillies used in this recipe, but where's the fun in that? Embrace the heat and make it sweat!

Serves 4

12 whole large prawns (shrimp)
6 kaffir lime leaves, torn in half
2 coriander (cilantro) roots, scraped clean, plus coriander leaves to garnish
1 lemongrass stalk, white part only, bruised, then cut into 2 cm (¾ in) lengths
7–8 thin slices galangal
5–6 Thai red chillies, bruised, then halved
1 tomato, quartered
100 g (3½ oz) straw mushrooms (see Note)
3 tablespoons fish sauce
3 tablespoons freshly squeezed lime juice
2 tablespoons Nam prik pao (see page 160)
2 teaspoons sugar

Peel and devein the prawns, reserving the heads and shells to make the broth.

Fill a large saucepan with 1.25 litres (42 fl oz/5 cups) water, add the prawn heads and shells and bring to the boil over medium heat. Simmer for 20–30 minutes, then strain the broth into a clean saucepan. Discard the shells but keep the heads for garnish.

Add the kaffir lime leaves, coriander roots, lemongrass, galangal and chilli to the broth and bring to the boil over medium–high heat. Boil for 3–4 minutes, until the fragrance from the broth fills the whole kitchen.

Add the tomato and mushrooms and bring the broth back to the boil. Add the prawns, then reduce the heat to medium–low and simmer for 2–3 minutes, until the prawns are just cooked. Add the fish sauce, lime juice, nam prik pao and sugar and stir to combine. Taste and adjust the seasoning accordingly.

To serve, ladle the soup into serving bowls and garnish with the prawn heads and coriander leaves.

Note: Fresh straw mushrooms can be hard to come by and are usually sold in tins. If you can't find any, just use button or oyster mushrooms instead.

BULDAK WITH CHEESE (KOREAN FIRE CHICKEN)

Buldak literally means 'fire chicken' and that is no exaggeration — it's super, super hot! In fact, this dish is so hot that some genius decided to tone down the spiciness by covering it in cheese. A lot of Koreans like to eat this dish as a 'mukbang' (filming yourself eating large amounts of food), to see if they can finish a huge bowlful in one sitting. So, do you accept the challenge?

Serves 4–6

1 kg (2 lb 3 oz) boneless skinless
  chicken thighs
2 tablespoons vegetable oil
250 g (9 oz) shredded mozzarella
1 spring onion (scallion), thinly sliced,
  to garnish
2 cos (romaine) or butter lettuces,
  leaves separated, to serve

Buldak chilli marinade
40 g (1½ oz/⅓ cup) gochugaru (see
  Note on page 98)
3 tablespoons gochujang (see Note
  on page 67)
2 tablespoons Korean rice
  syrup (ssalyeot; see Note on
  page 98) or corn syrup
1 tablespoon sugar
2 tablespoons soy sauce
1 tablespoon sesame oil
½ teaspoon freshly ground
  black pepper
5 garlic cloves, finely chopped
5 cm (2 in) knob of ginger, finely grated

To make the chilli marinade, combine the ingredients in a large bowl.

Trim any excess fat off the chicken, then cut into bite-sized pieces. Add the chicken to the marinade and mix until the chicken is completely coated. Cover and leave to marinate in the fridge for at least 1 hour.

Heat the vegetable oil in a wok or large frying pan over high heat. Add the chicken and marinade and stir-fry for 5 minutes. Add 60 ml (2 fl oz/¼ cup) water, reduce the heat to medium and simmer, covered, for another 5 minutes. Remove the lid, increase the heat to medium–high and stir continuously for 2–3 minutes, until the sauce has reduced and thickened.

Preheat the grill (broiler) to high.

Sprinkle half the cheese over the base of a heavy cast-iron pan, then place the chicken on top. Scatter the remaining cheese over the chicken and grill for 5 minutes or until the cheese begins to brown and blister.

Transfer the chicken to a serving platter and scatter the spring onion over the top. Invite guests to wrap the chicken in the lettuce leaves (like san choy bao) and dig in.

BLISTERING LA ZI JI

This dish is also known as hide-and-seek chicken because you have to rummage through an unconscionable amount of dried chillies to find the addictive morsels of crispy fried chicken. Please don't be a hero and start eating all the dried chillies on the plate, they are mostly there for flavour and not for consumption. Unless, of course, you want to say goodbye to your backside the next day, in which case, be my guest!

Serves 4

500 g (1 lb 2 oz) boneless chicken thighs, skin on
2 tablespoons sweet potato flour (see Note)
1 free-range egg white
vegetable oil, for frying
5 cm (2 in) knob of ginger, thinly sliced
5 garlic cloves, thinly sliced
2 teaspoons Sichuan peppercorns
20 dried Sichuan chillies, cut into 3 cm (1¼ in) lengths
1 tablespoon doubanjiang (see Note on page 26)
1 tablespoon Shaoxing rice wine
1 teaspoon sugar
1 tablespoon light soy sauce
2 teaspoons Sichuan chilli oil (see page 157)
3 spring onions (scallions), green part only, cut into 5 cm (2 in) lengths
1 teaspoon toasted sesame seeds

La zi ji marinade
1 teaspoon sea salt
1 tablespoon Shaoxing rice wine
5 cm (2 in) knob of ginger, thinly sliced
3 spring onions (scallions), white part only
1 teaspoon ground white pepper
½ teaspoon Sichuan peppercorns

Cut the chicken into bite-sized pieces, then transfer to a bowl. Add the marinade ingredients, mix everything together and set aside to marinate for 15 minutes.

Add the sweet potato flour and egg white to the chicken, then use your hands to rub the mixture into the chicken until well coated.

Heat 2.5 cm (1 in) of vegetable oil in a wok or large frying pan over medium heat to 165°C (330°F) on a kitchen thermometer. Fry the chicken and its marinade for 3 minutes, stirring occasionally. Remove the chicken using a wire-mesh strainer and set aside on a tray. Discard the spring onion.

Increase the heat to high and bring the oil's temperature to 190°C (380°F). Return the chicken to the wok or pan and flash-fry for 1–2 minutes, until the chicken is golden brown and crisp. Remove the chicken from the wok or pan and rest on a wire rack with paper towels underneath to soak up the excess oil.

Drain the fried chicken oil and give the wok or pan a wipe with paper towel. Now fill the wok with 125 ml (4 fl oz/½ cup) of fresh oil and bring to smoking point over medium–low heat. Add the ginger and fry for 1 minute, then add the garlic, Sichuan peppercorns and dried chillies and fry for 2 minutes or until fragrant and the garlic is crisp but not burnt. Add the doubanjiang and stir to mix well, then add the Shaoxing rice wine, sugar and soy sauce and cook for 3 minutes or until most of the liquid has evaporated. Return the chicken to the wok or pan along with the chilli oil and green spring onion. Give the wok or pan a few tosses, then transfer the mixture to a serving plate. Finally, sprinkle the sesame seeds over the chicken and serve.

Note: Sweet potato flour is also known as kamote flour. You can purchase it from most health-food stores and Asian supermarkets.

VOLCANIC VINDALOO

Beef vindaloo is a traditional curry from Goa, most notably famous for being one of India's hottest dishes. A good vindaloo should be a harmonious balance of sweet, sour and hot, and by hot I mean super hot! Try to maintain the chilli quantity when making this curry, but feel free to adjust the sweet and sour levels to your liking.

Serves 8

2 tablespoons vegetable oil

2 large onions, finely chopped

1 tomato, chopped

1.5 kg (3 lb 5 oz) chuck steak or gravy beef, cut into 2.5 cm (1 in) chunks

2 teaspoons sea salt

1 tablespoon sugar

steamed basmati rice or warm naan bread, to serve

raita, to serve

Vindaloo spice paste

2.5 cm (1 in) knob of ginger, sliced

1 long green chilli, sliced in half lengthways

2 teaspoons black mustard seeds

1 teaspoon fenugreek seeds

1 teaspoon fennel seeds

1 teaspoon cumin seeds

1 shard cassia bark or ¼ cinnamon stick

4 green cardamom pods

8 whole cloves

1 teaspoon black peppercorns

3 tablespoons Kashmiri chilli powder

1 teaspoon ground turmeric

1 tablespoon ground coriander

1½ tablespoons white vinegar

To make the vindaloo spice paste, place all the ingredients and 2 tablespoons water in a blender and process to a fine paste.

Heat the vegetable oil in a large saucepan over medium–high heat. Add the onion and sauté for 3–5 minutes, until soft and golden. Add the tomato and sauté for 2 minutes, then add the spice paste, reduce the heat to medium and cook, stirring frequently, for 10–15 minutes, until the spice paste has turned a dark-brown colour and the oil has rendered out. Add the beef, stir to combine and cook for 2 minutes to let the beef and spices get to know each other.

Add 250 ml (8½ fl oz/1 cup) water to the pan, then stir and bring to the boil. Season with the salt and sugar, then reduce the heat to medium–low and braise, covered but with the lid slightly ajar and stirring occasionally, for 2–3 hours until the beef is completely tender and the sauce is reduced and thick. Taste and adjust the seasonings if necessary.

Serve warm with steamed basmati rice or warm naan bread and some raita to counteract the heat of the vindaloo beef.

TTEOKBOKKI

You will find Tteokbokki on nearly every street corner in Korea. It's one of the country's most popular street foods and it's loved by everyone. With its chewy rice cakes doused in that deep red spicy sauce, Tteokbokki is a comforting and soul-satisfying dish. This recipe is a very typical Tteokbokki using inexpensive ingredients, but you can easily add a protein of your choice to make it a more substantial meal.

Serves 4–6

500 g (1 lb 2 oz) frozen tteok (Korean tubular rice cakes; see Note)
1 tablespoon olive oil
750 ml (25½ fl oz/3 cups) vegetable stock
2 Korean fish cake sheets, cut into bite-sized pieces (see Note)
2 spring onions (scallions), cut into 5 cm (2 in) lengths
toasted sesame seeds, to garnish

Tteokbokki sauce
3 garlic cloves, minced
2 tablespoons gochugaru (see Note on page 98)
100 g (3½ oz/⅓ cup) gochujang (see Note on page 67)
1 tablespoon soy sauce
1 tablespoon sugar
2 teaspoons sesame oil

Separate the frozen tteok into individual pieces, then soak them in warm water for 20 minutes to soften. Drain, then place the tteok in a bowl and toss with the olive oil until well coated so they don't stick together.

Pour the vegetable stock into a large deep frying pan over medium–high heat. Add the tteokbokki sauce ingredients, stir well to combine and bring to the boil. Add the ttoek and cook, stirring frequently, for 8–10 minutes, until the rice cakes are very soft and the sauce is reduced and thick.

Add the fish cake pieces to the pan, then reduce the heat to medium and simmer for 5 minutes. Taste and adjust the seasoning if needed. Add the spring onion, give everything a final stir, then transfer the stew to a serving dish. Sprinkle sesame seeds over the top and serve immediately.

Note: Frozen tteok and fish cake sheets are popular Korean ingredients that can be found at any Korean supermarket.

KOREAN FIRE NOODLES

This recipe is not rocket science, but more of a challenge for those cocky chilli fanatics who always say, 'This dish isn't hot!' One rule is that you are not allowed to touch the glass of milk until you finish all the noodles in the bowl. Just don't go crying to your mama the next day ...

〇〇〇〇〇〇〇〇〇〇〇〇〇〇〇〇〇〇〇〇〇〇〇〇〇〇〇〇〇

Serves 2

2 packets instant ramen or
   udon noodles
large handful of shredded iceberg
   lettuce leaves (optional)
fried shallots, to garnish
2 free-range eggs, fried sunny side up
glasses of milk, on standby

Fire noodle sauce
1 tablespoon vegetable oil
2 tablespoons gochujang (see Note
   on page 67)
2 teaspoons Korean capsaicin
   hot sauce (see Note on page 93)
2 tablespoons light soy sauce
1 tablespoon dark soy sauce
2 teaspoons rice vinegar
3 garlic cloves, minced
2.5 cm (1 in) knob of ginger, grated
2 teaspoons sesame oil
1 tablespoon caster (superfine) sugar

To make the fire noodle sauce, combine the ingredients in a bowl and stir until the sugar has dissolved. Set aside.

Cook the instant noodles according to the packet instructions, then drain, saving 125 ml (4 fl oz/½ cup) of the cooking water. Divide the noodles between two serving bowls.

Add 2 tablespoons of the fire noodle sauce to each bowl and toss until the noodles are well coated. Top with the shredded lettuce (if using) and fried shallots, and finish with the fried eggs.

Serve with glasses of milk to reduce the burn!

MA LA XIANG GUO

A new invention from China that has all the cool kids raving, this ridiculously spicy vegetarian dish has taken the world by storm. Its origins are unknown, but the distinctive numbing sensation from the Sichuan peppercorns is unmistakably addictive.

ooo o o o ooo o o o o o o o o o o o o o o o o o o o o o

Serves 4

30 g (1 oz) dried wood-ear mushrooms
2 celery stalks, thinly sliced diagonally
1 large carrot, thinly sliced diagonally
2 potatoes, peeled and thinly sliced
50 g (1¾ oz) shiitake mushrooms, sliced
300 g (10½ oz) fresh lotus root, peeled and thinly sliced
2 cm (¾ in) knob of ginger, sliced into thin matchsticks
5 garlic cloves, thinly sliced
10–20 dried Sichuan chillies, deseeded and cut into 2 cm (¾ in) lengths
1 tablespoon Sichuan peppercorns
2 tablespoons doubanjiang (see Note on page 26)
1 tablespoon Shaoxing rice wine
350 g (12½ oz) firm tofu, thinly sliced
sea salt
1 tablespoon toasted sesame seeds
80 g (2¾ oz/½ cup) roasted peanuts
3 spring onions (scallions), cut into 5 cm (2 in) lengths
handful of garlic chives, snipped

Spice-infused oil
80 ml (2½ fl oz/⅓ cup) vegetable oil
3–4 star anise
2 tablespoons Sichuan peppercorns
1 black cardamom pod
4 green cardamom pods
1 whole nutmeg

Soak the wood-ear mushrooms in hot water for 1 hour, then drain and cut into bite-sized pieces, discarding any hard bits.

Meanwhile, bring a large saucepan of salted water to a rolling boil over medium–high heat. Add the celery, carrot, potato, shiitake mushroom and lotus root and blanch for 2 minutes. Drain and set aside.

To make the spice-infused oil, heat the oil in a wok or small saucepan over low heat. Add the remaining ingredients and gently cook for 30 minutes or until the spices are very fragrant and starting to brown. Use a slotted spoon to scoop out the spices and discard.

Heat the spice-infused oil in a wok or large frying pan over medium–high heat. Add the ginger, garlic, chilli and Sichuan peppercorns and stir-fry for 30 seconds or until fragrant. Add the doubanjiang, Shaoxing rice wine, blanched vegetables, wood-ear mushroom and tofu and stir-fry for 1 minute or until well combined. Season with salt, then toss through the sesame seeds, roasted peanuts, spring onion and garlic chives. Serve immediately.

FEROCIOUS PHAAL

Behold! I present to you the hottest mutha f*ckin' curry of them all — the phaal. This deadly dish originates not from India, but a Bangladeshi restaurant in Birmingham, UK. It is so notoriously spicy that the chef has to wear a gas mask to cook it, and it has reportedly left diners vomiting and crying. The recipe is still a closely guarded secret, but my version shows no mercy either. This is not for the faint-hearted!

Serves 4

1 kg (2 lb 3 oz) boneless lamb leg, cut into bite-sized pieces
2 tablespoons ground cumin
3 tablespoons ground coriander
1 teaspoon chilli powder
3 scotch bonnet chillies
5 long green chillies or jalapeno chillies
2 tablespoons vegetable oil
5 cm (2 in) knob of ginger, grated
5 garlic cloves, finely chopped
1 red onion, halved, then each half cut into quarters
2 teaspoons chilli flakes
2 teaspoons freshly ground black pepper
2 tablespoons tomato paste (concentrated purée)
400 g (14 oz) tin diced tomatoes
1 tablespoon sugar
2 teaspoons sea salt
1 teaspoon kasoori methi (see Note on page 33)
handful of coriander (cilantro) leaves, finely chopped
steamed basmati rice and warm naan bread, to serve

Place the lamb, half the cumin, 1 tablespoon of the ground coriander and the chilli powder in a bowl and use your hands to mix everything together until the lamb is well coated. Cover and set aside to marinate in the fridge for at least 2 hours, but preferably overnight.

Wearing kitchen gloves, place the scotch bonnets, green chillies and 2 tablespoons water in a blender and blitz to a smooth, watery paste. Open all the windows in the kitchen and turn on the extractor fan if you have one (this next step might sting a little!).

Heat the vegetable oil in a large saucepan over medium–high heat. Add the ginger and garlic and sauté for 1 minute or until fragrant. Add the onion and sauté for 2 minutes or until soft and translucent. Add 2 tablespoons water to the pan, stir, then add the chilli flakes, 2 tablespoons of the chilli paste (trust me, you don't need more!) and cook for 1 minute. Add the remaining cumin and ground coriander, the black pepper and another 2 tablespoons water, then stir and cook until the water has evaporated. Add the tomato paste, tomatoes, sugar and the salt, then stir until combined. Let the mixture slowly bubble for 10 minutes until the sauce has thickened to a gravy.

Add the lamb to the curry sauce and stir until well coated. Reduce the heat to low and simmer, stirring occasionally, for 1½ hours or until the meat is cooked through and tender. If the sauce starts to dry out during cooking, add 2 tablespoons water at a time. Taste and adjust the seasonings if necessary, then sprinkle in the kasoori methi and coriander and give everything a quick stir.

Serve with steamed basmati rice, warm naan bread and lots of milk or a lassi on standby. You've been warned!

FIRESTARTER PIZZA

Nothing beats a freshly made pizza from scratch, especially one that sets your mouth on fire! Load up this pizza with as much meat, cheese and jalapenos as your stomach can handle, but leave out the pineapple ...

○ ○

Makes 2

1 tablespoon olive oil
2 pork and fennel sausages, casings
   removed
½ teaspoon cayenne pepper
1 pepperoni, thinly sliced
15 cherry tomatoes, halved
2–3 jalapeno chillies, thinly sliced
½ red onion, thinly sliced
100 g (3½ oz/1 cup) shredded
   mozzarella

Pizza dough
1 teaspoon instant dried yeast
25 g (¾ oz) caster (superfine) sugar
320 ml (11 fl oz) lukewarm water
500 g (1 lb 2 oz) strong '00' flour, plus
   extra for dusting
2 teaspoons sea salt
60 ml (2 fl oz/¼ cup) olive oil, plus
   extra for greasing
fine semolina, for dusting

To make the pizza dough, combine the yeast, sugar and water in a jug, stir well and set aside for 5–10 minutes to activate the yeast.

Combine the flour and salt in a stand mixer with the dough hook attached. With the mixer running on low speed, add the yeast mixture and olive oil and mix until a smooth ball forms. Alternatively, to make the dough by hand, combine the flour and salt in a large bowl. Make a well in the centre and pour in the yeast mixture and oil. Using your hands, bring the mixture together to form a rough dough. Transfer to a lightly floured work surface and knead for 10 minutes or until you have a smooth and elastic ball of dough.

Transfer the dough to a lightly greased bowl, cover and set aside in a warm place for 1 hour or until doubled in size.

Meanwhile, make the pizza sauce. Heat the olive oil in a large frying pan over medium–high heat. Add the garlic and chilli flakes and sauté for 1 minute or until fragrant. Add the pizza sauce and sriracha, stir well and simmer for 5 minutes or until slightly reduced. Remove from the heat and set aside.

Heat the olive oil in another large frying pan over medium–high heat. Add the sausage meat and use the back of a wooden spoon

Pizza sauce

1 tablespoon olive oil
3 garlic cloves, minced
1 teaspoon chilli flakes
250 ml (8½ fl oz/1 cup) store-bought
    pizza sauce
1 tablespoon Sriracha hot sauce
    (see page 158 or use store-bought)

to roughly chop the sausage into smaller chunks. Add the cayenne pepper and cook, stirring frequently, for 3 minutes or until the sausage is well browned. Transfer the sausage to a bowl.

Preheat the oven to its highest setting and place a pizza stone on the middle shelf.

Tip the dough onto a lightly floured work surface and knead a few times to shape the dough back into a ball. Cut the dough ball in half.

Working with one piece of dough at a time, use your hands to stretch the dough into a 22 cm (8¾ in) round pizza base, about 5 mm (¼ in) thick. Sprinkle a handful of semolina on a baking tray and place the pizza base on top. Spread a ladleful of pizza sauce over the base, then top with half the sausage mince, pepperoni, tomato, jalapeno and red onion. Liberally sprinkle half the cheese over the top.

Very carefully slide the pizza onto the very hot pizza stone and cook for 10–15 minutes, until the pizza base is golden and the toppings are slightly charred. While this pizza is cooking, prepare the second one.

Rest the pizzas for a couple of minutes, then slice up and consume with cold beer.

NUMBING
PAD PRIK NUA

In Thai, pad prik means stir-fried with chilli. This popular and economical method of cooking is considered 'fast food' in Thailand, and many white-collar workers in Bangkok enjoy pad prik nua for lunch, perhaps to relieve stress through a good chilli workout. If you want to experience the real heat of an authentic Thai dish, then don't skimp on the amount of Thai chillies used in this recipe.

Serves 2

2–3 long red chillies, roughly chopped
4–5 Thai red chillies, roughly chopped
2 tablespoons vegetable oil
3 garlic cloves, thinly sliced
300 g (10½ oz) beef sirloin, thinly sliced
    against the grain
½ red capsicum (bell pepper), cut into
    thin strips
2 tablespoons palm sugar
2 tablespoons fish sauce
1 tablespoon oyster sauce
1 tablespoon cornflour (corn
    starch), mixed with 60 ml
    (2 fl oz/¼ cup) water
large handful of basil leaves
steamed jasmine rice, to serve

Place the chillies and 1 tablespoon water in a mortar and pestle and pound to a rough paste.

Heat the vegetable oil in a wok or large frying pan over medium–high heat until smoking hot. Add the chilli paste and garlic and stir-fry for 1 minute or until fragrant. Add the beef and stir-fry for 1 minute, then add the capsicum and stir-fry for another minute. Add the sugar, fish sauce, oyster sauce and cornflour mixture and stir well to combine. Simmer for 1 minute until the sauce thickens, then add the basil leaves and stir through.

Serve with steamed jasmine rice on the side.

SEARING JERK CHICKEN

Jerk is a style of cooking native to Jamaica. The name refers to the spice rub, wet marinade and the specific cooking technique. The three key ingredients in jerk seasoning are allspice, thyme and extremely hot scotch bonnet chillies. How many chillies you use in this recipe is, of course, totally up to you, but jerk chicken should definitely make your lips tingle and your mouth numb; if it doesn't, then you just ain't doing it right.

Serves 4

1.5 kg (3 lb 5 oz) whole chicken, cut
    into 8 pieces
vegetable oil, for greasing
3 limes, halved and charred
steamed rice mixed with black beans
    or fried plantains, to serve (optional)

Jerk marinade
1 tablespoon sea salt
2 teaspoons freshly ground
    black pepper
1 large onion, chopped
3 spring onions (scallions), chopped
1 tablespoon thyme leaves
2 tablespoons vegetable oil
2 tablespoons ground allspice
1 teaspoon ground cinnamon
1 teaspoon ground nutmeg
5 cm (2 in) knob of ginger, grated
2 teaspoons dark brown sugar
80 ml (2½ fl oz/⅓ cup) freshly squeezed
    lime juice
60 ml (2 fl oz/¼ cup) rice vinegar
2 scotch bonnet chillies, chopped
5 garlic cloves, chopped

To make the jerk marinade, place the ingredients in a food processor and blend to a smooth paste. (Make sure you wear kitchen gloves before handling the scotch bonnet chillies as they are VERY hot.)

Place the chicken in a large bowl and pour the jerk marinade over the top. Put your kitchen gloves on again, then rub the marinade into the chicken until nicely coated. Cover and set aside in the fridge to marinate for at least 2 hours, but preferably overnight.

Preheat a barbecue grill plate to high and grease the grill with vegetable oil.

Reduce the heat to medium, then remove the chicken from the marinade and place it on the grill. Cook, turning frequently and basting with the left-over marinade, for 20 minutes or until the chicken is cooked through and the skin is nicely charred.

Transfer the chicken to a serving platter, along with the charred lime. If you like, serve the chicken with steamed rice mixed with black beans or, more traditionally, with fried plantains.

BLISTERING
BUDAE JJIGAE

Budae jjigae is the ultimate winter warming stew to eat during the cooler months. The dish was created shortly after the armistice that ended the Korean War, using the scrounged or smuggled surplus foods from US army bases, hence its Western name 'army base stew'. Cold beer is highly recommended to accompany this extremely spicy bowl of goodness!

Serves 4–6

200 g (7 oz/1 cup) kimchi, roughly
   chopped
200 g (7 oz) SPAM, thinly sliced
2 Frankfurt sausages, sliced diagonally
300 g (10½ oz) firm tofu, sliced into
   1 cm (½ in) thick strips (optional)
200 g (7 oz) shiitake mushrooms,
   thinly sliced
50 g (1¾ oz) enoki mushrooms, roots
   trimmed
50 g (1¾ oz) frozen tteok (Korean
   tubular rice cakes; see Note),
   soaked in warm water for
   20 minutes, drained
1 litre (34 fl oz/4 cups) vegetable stock
2 spring onions (scallions), thinly sliced
110 g (4 oz) instant ramen noodles
1–2 slices stretchy cheese, such as
   mozzarella or American yellow
steamed rice, to serve

Budae jjigae chilli paste
3 garlic cloves, minced
2 tablespoons gochugaru (see Note)
1 tablespoon gochujang (see Note)
2 tablespoons mirin rice wine
1 tablespoon soy sauce
1 teaspoon sesame oil
2 teaspoons sugar

To make the budae jjigae chilli paste, combine the ingredients in a bowl. Set aside.

Arrange the kimchi, spam, sausage, tofu (if using), mushrooms and tteok around the base of a shallow flameproof casserole dish. Spoon the chilli paste into the centre of the dish, then pour the vegetable stock around the chilli paste. Cover, bring to the boil over medium–high heat and cook for 5–8 minutes.

Gently stir the chilli paste into the broth and sprinkle the spring onion over the top. Place the ramen noodles in the dish, then place the cheese slices on top of the noodles. Let the stew simmer for 2–3 minutes, until the noodles are cooked. Remove from the heat and take the dish to the table.

If you have a portable gas burner, serve the hot stew over the burner at the table so it remains steaming hot.

Serve the stew with steamed rice to soak up that spicy sauce.

Note: Frozen tteok, gochugaru and gochujang can be purchased from Korean supermarkets.

DIABLO
DRUNKEN SHRIMP

The name says it all. These Cajun-style fiery prawns (shrimp) are made even more delicious by swimming in a pool of buttery, boozy liquid gold. The Old Bay Seasoning is crucial to bring out Louisiana's Cajun flavours, while the heat from the chilli and the bitterness of the beer really elevate the sweetness of the prawns. Serve with plenty of bread to soak up the addictive sauce.

Serves 4

1 kg (2 lb 3 oz) raw prawns (shrimp), peeled and deveined with tails left intact
2 teaspoons sea salt
3 tablespoons Old Bay Seasoning
3 tablespoons olive oil
5 garlic cloves, finely chopped
1 red habanero chilli, finely chopped
1 teaspoon cayenne pepper
2 teaspoons smoked paprika
250 ml (8½ fl oz/1 cup) beer of your choice, such as IPA or pale ale, plus an extra splash to serve
60 g (2 oz/¼ cup) cold butter, cut into small cubes
freshly ground black pepper
parsley leaves, finely chopped, to serve
bread rolls, to serve

Combine the prawns, salt and 1 tablespoon of the Old Bay Seasoning in a bowl and mix until the prawns are well coated.

Heat 2 tablespoons of the olive oil in a cast-iron pan over medium-high heat. Add the prawns and sauté for 3 minutes or until just pink and cooked through. Transfer to a plate and set aside.

To the same pan, add the remaining oil and reduce the heat to medium-low. Add the garlic, chilli, cayenne pepper, paprika and remaining Old Bay Seasoning and cook for 1 minute. Pour half the beer into the pan and stir to deglaze, scraping up any caramelised bits stuck to the base of the pan. Add the remaining beer, increase the heat to medium and simmer for 3–4 minutes, until the sauce has reduced by half. Whisk in the butter, a little at a time, until the sauce is glossy and thick. Season to taste with salt and pepper.

Return the prawns to the pan and gently stir until well coated in that glorious sauce. Simmer for 1 minute, then remove from the heat. Sprinkle with parsley and add a final splash of beer for good luck.

Serve with bread rolls.

NACHOS FROM HELL

Let all hell break loose with these devilish nachos! It's the slow burning sensation after every mouthful that keeps you coming back for more and shovelling another spicy hot tortilla chip into your gob. Serve with several bottles of ice-cold beer to help keep that fiery sensation at bay.

Serves 6–8

250 g (9 oz) tortilla chips
200 g (7 oz/2 cups) shredded
    cheddar
250 g (9 oz/1 cup) Hot salsa
    (see page 162)
1 large semi-ripe avocado, diced
2 jalapeno chillies, thinly sliced
handful of coriander (cilantro) leaves,
    to serve

Mexican grilled chicken
400 g (14 oz) boneless skinless
    chicken thighs
3 garlic cloves, minced
1 tablespoon olive oil
1 teaspoon ground cumin
1 teaspoon smoked paprika
1 teaspoon cayenne pepper
1 teaspoon sea salt
1 teaspoon freshly ground
    black pepper

To make the Mexican grilled chicken, place the ingredients in a bowl and use your hands to massage the spices and oil into the chicken until nicely coated. Cover and set aside in the fridge to marinate for at least 1 hour, but preferably overnight.

Preheat a barbecue grill to high.

Grill the chicken for 3–4 minutes on each side until cooked through and lightly charred all over. Transfer the chicken to a chopping board, rest for 5 minutes, then cut into small pieces. Set aside.

Preheat the oven to 200°C (400°F).

To make the nachos cheese, melt the butter in a saucepan over medium heat. When the butter starts to foam, slowly sprinkle the flour into the pan, whisking constantly to prevent the flour from burning, until you have a thick paste. Continue to whisk and slowly pour the milk into the flour mixture in a thin, steady stream, until the mixture is well combined without any lumps. Keep whisking for 5 minutes or until the sauce thickens and resembles thick cream. Add the cheese and whisk until it melts into the sauce. Add the hot sauce and Carolina reaper chilli and stir to combine. Taste and season with salt and pepper, then remove from the heat, cover and keep warm.

Nachos cheese

60 g (2 oz/¼ cup) unsalted butter
35 g (1¼ oz/¼ cup) plain
　(all-purpose) flour
500 ml (17 fl oz/2 cups) full-
　cream (whole) milk
200 g (7 oz) grated sharp cheddar
2　tablespoons hot sauce, such
　as Tabasco, Frank's, RedHot or
　Sriracha hot sauce (see page 158
　or use store-bought)
1　Carolina reaper chilli, finely chopped
sea salt and freshly ground
　black pepper

Spread half the tortilla chips in the base of a baking dish. Top with the Mexican chicken, then drizzle over some of the nachos cheese. Add the remaining tortilla chips and scatter over the cheddar. Bake in the oven for 8–10 minutes, until the cheese is melted and blistering.

Drizzle the nachos with extra nachos cheese, followed by the hot salsa. Garnish with the avocado, jalapeno and coriander leaves, and serve immediately.

HOT SATAY SAUCE

I forbid you to use peanut butter to make a satay sauce! It's so easy to make a good spicy satay sauce from scratch. Not only is it a quintessential dipping sauce for chicken skewers (see page 54), you can also add it to stir-fried noodles or use it as a salad dressing. Delicious and versatile!

Makes about 450 g (1 lb)

160 g (5½ oz/1 cup) raw peanuts, skins removed
125 ml (4 fl oz/½ cup) peanut oil
1 tablespoon kecap manis
2 tablespoons sugar
½ teaspoon sea salt
1 tablespoon tamarind concentrate

Satay spice paste
8–10 dried red chillies, deseeded and soaked in hot water for 10 minutes
3 garlic cloves, peeled
6–8 French shallots, roughly chopped
2 lemongrass stalks, white part only, roughly chopped
2 cm (¾ in) knob of ginger, roughly chopped
2 cm (¾ in) knob of galangal, roughly chopped

Toast the peanuts in a frying pan over low heat, stirring occasionally, for 10 minutes or until they are golden brown. Remove from the heat and leave to cool completely. Transfer the peanuts to a food processor and pulse until roughly crushed. Set aside.

To make the spice paste, drain the chillies, reserving 60 ml (2 fl oz/¼ cup) of the soaking water. Place the chillies and reserved water, along with all the other spice paste ingredients in a food processor or blender and blitz to a fine paste.

Heat the peanut oil in a wok or large frying pan over medium heat. Fry the spice paste, stirring regularly, for 8–10 minutes, until the oil has split from the paste and the mixture is fragrant and dark brown in colour. Add the kecap manis, sugar, salt, tamarind concentrate, crushed peanuts and 250 ml (8½ fl oz/1 cup) water to the pan, reduce the heat to low and cook, stirring occasionally, for 10 minutes. Taste and adjust the seasoning if needed.

The satay sauce will keep in a jar in the fridge for up to 1 week.

SAMBAL BELACHAN

Sambal belachan is an indispensable chilli condiment in Malaysian cuisine. It is an essential accompaniment to the national dish nasi lemak, but is also used in other recipes, such as the sambal-fried boiled eggs on page 63. Don't be put off by the smell of the belachan, it is absolutely delicious once cooked.

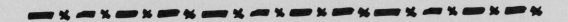

Makes about 260 g (9 oz)

100 g (3½ oz) dried red chillies, soaked
    in hot water for 10 minutes
20 g (¾ oz) belachan shrimp paste
    (see Note)
4–5 long red chillies, roughly chopped
2.5 cm (1 in) knob of ginger, sliced
50 g (1¾ oz) French shallots
5 garlic cloves
2 teaspoons sea salt
1 tablespoon sugar
250 ml (8½ fl oz/1 cup) vegetable oil

Drain the chillies, reserving 125 ml (4 fl oz/½ cup) of the soaking water.

Wrap the shrimp paste tightly in foil and place in a frying pan over medium heat. Toast the shrimp paste, flipping occasionally, for 5 minutes or until fragrant. (It is important to have the kitchen well ventilated as the shrimp paste can be very pungent and the smell will linger in the air for days. You've been warned!) Remove from the heat and set aside to cool completely before removing the foil. The shrimp paste should be dry and crumbly.

Place the shrimp paste in a food processor with the drained chillies and 60 ml (2 fl oz/¼ cup) of the reserved soaking water. Add the remaining ingredients except the vegetable oil and blend to a fine paste. Add a little more of the reserved soaking water if the paste seems very dry.

Heat the oil in a wok or large frying pan over medium heat. Add the chilli paste and cook, stirring regularly, for 15 minutes or until the oil has split from the paste and the sambal is dark red in colour. Remove from the heat and set aside to cool completely.

The sambal will keep in an airtight container in the fridge for up to 6 months.

Note: Belachan is a Malaysian fermented shrimp paste used in many Southeast Asian dishes. It is available at most Asian supermarkets.

REMPAH
SPICE PASTE

The Malay word 'rempah' means spice paste. It is an essential blend of herbs and spices used as an aromatic foundation for a whole host of dishes in Malaysian and Singaporean cuisine, including curry laksa (see page 74) and Malaysian chicken curry (see page 106). It's best to only make enough for the recipe you are cooking and use it immediately while still fresh.

Makes about 350 g (12½ oz)

20 g (¾ oz) belachan shrimp paste (see Note on page 155)

10 g (⅓ oz) dried red chillies, soaked in hot water for 30 minutes, drained

5 long red chillies, deseeded and roughly chopped

10 g (⅓ oz) candlenuts, roasted (see Note)

100 g (3½ oz) French shallots

15 g (½ oz) fresh turmeric, peeled and roughly chopped

2 lemongrass stalks, white part only, roughly chopped

Wrap the shrimp paste tightly in foil and place in a frying pan over medium heat. Toast the shrimp paste, flipping occasionally, for 5 minutes or until fragrant. Remove from the heat and set aside to cool completely before removing the foil. The shrimp paste should be dry and crumbly.

Place the toasted shrimp paste and the remaining ingredients in a food processor and blitz to a fine paste. If the mixture is very dry, add a tablespoon of water to get the food processor going.

Use the spice paste immediately to make the curry laksa on page 74.

Note: Candlenuts are traditionally used in spice pastes in Southeast Asian cuisines. They are available from most Asian supermarkets, but macadamia nuts can be substituted if you can't find them.

SICHUAN CHILLI OIL

This stuff is addictive and I use it on almost everything! It is important to use Sichuan chilli flakes in this recipe as they lend a nice toasty flavour and also give the oil that characteristic vivid red colour. It is a must with the pork dumplings on page 80, but also excellent drizzled over noodles and fried rice. Make extra because it won't last!

Makes about 500 ml (17 fl oz/2 cups)

60 g (2 oz/½ cup) Sichuan chilli flakes (see Note)

1 tablespoon Sichuan peppercorns, coarsely ground, plus 1 teaspoon whole Sichuan peppercorns

2 teaspoons sea salt

500 ml (17 fl oz/2cups) canola or vegetable oil

5–6 garlic cloves, unpeeled

5 cm (2 in) knob of ginger, thickly sliced

3 star anise

1 teaspoon coriander seeds

1 cinnamon stick

5 green cardamom pods, smashed

2 black cardamom pods, smashed

1 tablespoon white sesame seeds, toasted

60 ml (2 fl oz/¼ cup) sesame oil

Place the chilli flakes, coarsely ground Sichuan peppercorns and salt in a heatproof bowl or jug and set aside.

Heat the oil in a heavy-based saucepan over very low heat. Add the garlic, ginger, star anise, coriander seeds, cinnamon, cardamom pods and whole Sichuan peppercorns and gently infuse in the oil for at least 1 hour or until very fragrant. Don't let the garlic or ginger burn or the oil will be bitter.

Using a wire-mesh strainer, remove the spices from the oil and discard. Increase the heat to high and when the oil starts to smoke very carefully and a little at a time, pour the hot oil into the dried chilli flake mixture. Add the sesame seeds and sesame oil, stir and set aside to completely cool. Store the chilli oil in a glass jar in the pantry for up to 3 months.

Note: Sichuan chilli flakes are made by frying the whole chillies and then grinding them into flakes. The frying enhances the flavour and vivid red colour of the Sichuan chilli oil. Sichuan chilli flakes are available at Asian supermarkets.

SRIRACHA HOT SAUCE

If you love sriracha chilli sauce then why not try and make your own? Not only is it easy to make, it means you can adjust the heat levels to suit your tastes (in other words you can make it spicier!). Plus you can make loads of it, so you always have some on hand to spice up any dish.

Makes about 500 ml (17 fl oz/2 cups)

700 g (1 lb 9 oz) red chillies, such as jalapeno, Thai or cow horn
3 garlic cloves, peeled
3 tablespoons light brown sugar
1 tablespoon sea salt
125 ml (4 fl oz/½ cup) white vinegar

Place the chillies, garlic, sugar, salt and 2 tablespoons water in a food processor and process to a fine purée. Pour the purée into a glass jar, cover with plastic wrap and leave in a cool dark spot for 5 days. Each day, take the purée out, skim off any foam that's formed on the surface and give the purée a stir.

Pour the fermented chilli mixture into a small saucepan, add the vinegar and bring to the boil over medium heat. Reduce the heat to low and simmer for 5–10 minutes, until the sauce has reduced to your desired consistency. (It's normal for it to be a little runny, as it will thicken up once it cools down.) Remove from the heat and set aside to cool. Pour the mixture into a food processor and blend to a smooth purée.

Using the back of a spatula, pass the mixture through a fine sieve into a bowl, pressing to squeeze as much liquid out as possible. Taste and adjust the seasoning if necessary. If the sauce seems too thick, add a little water and stir it through.

Once completely cool, store in an airtight container in the fridge, where it will keep for up to 6 months (if there's any left by then!).

ARRABBIATA
SAUCE

This spicy tomato sauce is your one-stop shop for all your Italian cooking needs. I will probably be scorned by Italian nonnas for using fish sauce in this recipe, but, trust me, it adds an amazing umami element to the sauce and intensifies the flavour.

Makes about 1 litre (34 fl oz/4 cups)

80 ml (2½ fl oz/⅓ cup) extra virgin olive oil
2 large onions, finely chopped
8 garlic cloves, finely chopped
5 teaspoons chilli flakes
40 g (1¾ oz) tomato paste (concentrated purée)
800 g (1 lb 12 oz) tinned diced tomatoes
1 tablespoon fish sauce
375 ml (12½ fl oz/1½ cups) vegetable stock
large handful of basil leaves, roughly chopped
sea salt

Heat the olive oil in a large saucepan over medium heat. Add the onion and sauté for 3 minutes or until soft and translucent. Add the garlic and chilli flakes and sauté for 2 minutes or until fragrant.

Add the tomato paste and cook, stirring, for 1 minute until well coated. Add the diced tomatoes, fish sauce and vegetable stock, then stir and bring to a simmer. Reduce the heat to low and cook, stirring occasionally, for 30 minutes or until the sauce has thickened and reduced slightly. Add the basil and simmer for a further 10 minutes. Taste and season accordingly with salt.

You can use the sauce immediately or set aside to cool completely, then store in an airtight container in the fridge for up to 1 week or in the freezer for up to 3 months.

NAM PRIK PAO

Nam prik pao is a common and versatile chilli paste used in Thai cuisine. It is a pantry staple in Thai households, and you simply can't cook tom yum goong (see page 121) without it. It can also be used as a condiment to add chilli heat to many noodle and rice dishes. I guarantee this paste will be your new best friend.

○ ○

Makes about 260 g (9 oz)

20 g (¾ oz) belachan shrimp paste (see Note on page 155)

12 large dried red chillies, deseeded (keep half the seeds in if you like it really hot)

20 g (¾ oz) dried shrimp, soaked in hot water for 10 minutes, drained

6 garlic cloves, roughly chopped

5–6 Asian shallots, roughly chopped

1 tablespoon fish sauce

2 tablespoons tamarind concentrate, mixed with 2 tablespoons water

80 g (2¾ oz) palm sugar, finely grated

60 ml (2 fl oz/¼ cup) vegetable oil, plus extra for drizzling

Wrap the shrimp paste tightly in foil and place in a frying pan over medium heat. Toast the shrimp paste, flipping occasionally, for 5 minutes or until fragrant. Remove from the heat and set aside to cool completely before removing the foil. The shrimp paste should be dry and crumbly.

Toast the chillies in the same frying pan over medium heat for 3 minutes or until starting to char at the edges. Be careful not to burn them, otherwise they will taste bitter. Remove from the heat and set aside. Next, toast the dried shrimp for 3 minutes or until fragrant and starting to char at the edges. Set aside with the dried chillies.

Place the shrimp paste, dried chillies, dried shrimp, garlic, shallot, fish sauce, tamarind mixture and palm sugar in a food processor and blend to a fine paste. Drizzle in a little vegetable oil to get the mixture going if necessary.

Heat the oil in a wok or frying pan over medium heat. Add the chilli paste and cook, stirring regularly, for 10–15 minutes, until it is mostly thick and dark brown in colour. Remove from the heat and set aside to cool completely. The paste should be the consistency of jam once it has cooled.

Store the nam prik pao in a jar in the fridge for up to 6 months.

HARISSA

Harissa is a fiery North African chilli paste that is super easy to make. Roasting the capsicums (bell peppers) over a naked flame helps to infuse a smoky sweetness to the chilli paste that makes it thoroughly delicious. Harissa goes really well with grilled meats and fish, or it can be used as a condiment, dressing, marinade or even a dip.

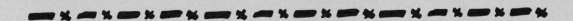

Makes about 270 g (9½ oz)

2 red capsicums (bell peppers)
5 garlic cloves, roughly chopped
2 tablespoons tomato paste
     (concentrated purée)
1 tablespoon smoked paprika
2 long red chillies, roughly chopped
1 red habanero chilli, roughly chopped
125 ml (4 fl oz/½ cup) olive oil
1 teaspoon sea salt
juice of ½ lemon

Harissa spice mix
1 tablespoon cumin seeds
1 teaspoon fennel seeds
2 teaspoons coriander seeds
2 teaspoons chilli flakes

To make the harissa spice mix, toast the spices in a dry frying pan over medium heat for 2 minutes or until fragrant. Transfer to a mortar and pestle and grind to a powder.

Roast the capsicums directly over a naked flame on the stovetop, flipping regularly, until charred and blackened on all sides. Alternatively, you can char them on a barbecue grill plate preheated to high. Place the charred capsicums in a zip-lock bag (be careful, they will be very hot!), seal the bag and set aside. Once the capsicums are cool enough to handle, peel and discard the charred skins and place the flesh in a food processor.

Add the ground spice mix and remaining ingredients to the roast capsicums and process until smooth. Taste and adjust the seasonings if necessary.

Store the harissa in a jar in the fridge for up to 1 month.

HOT SALSA

When done right, a well-made salsa makes an awesome addition to any number of dishes. To make a good salsa you need to use the best and freshest ingredients you can find to make the flavours really sing. As there is no cooking involved, salsa can be whipped up in minutes. It is refreshing yet bold and hot, and a must have with the nachos from hell on page 150.

Makes about 500 ml (17 fl oz/2 cup)

3 truss or roma tomatoes, cored
    and quartered
3 garlic cloves
2 jalapeno chillies, roughly chopped
1 red habanero chilli, roughly chopped
2 teaspoons ground cumin
1 tablespoon freshly squeezed
    lime juice
1½ teaspoons sea salt
½ red onion, finely diced
large handful of coriander (cilantro)
    leaves, roughly chopped
1 long green chilli, thinly sliced

Place the tomato, garlic, jalapeno and habanero chillies, ground cumin, lime juice and salt in a food processor. Pulse until the mixture resembles a chunky purée.

Transfer the mixture to a bowl and add the onion, coriander leaves and green chilli. Stir everything together, then taste and adjust the seasoning if necessary.

Refrigerate until ready to serve.

INDEX